# Colours of my Life

## Malcolm Allison

**Written with his close friend,
Daily Express soccer writer
JAMES LAWTON**

EVEREST BOOKS LIMITED
4 Valentine Place, London SE1

Published in Great Britain by Everest Books Ltd, 1975
ISBN 0903925 559
Copyright © Malcolm Allison and James Lawton 1975

Caricature of Malcolm Allison by Roy
Ullyett, specially commissioned by
Everest Books.

Computer typeset by Input Typesetting Limited. 4 Valentine Place. SE1.
Printed and bound in Great Britain by
Redwood Burn Limited, Trowbridge & Esher

# Contents

# Introduction
## by James Lawton

Malcolm Allison is a man of vast natural resources. At 47 years of age and minus one lung, he lives at a pace which would leave your average Chelsea swinger about as vital as a crumpled daisy; he retains the build and the carriage of the great American quarter-back, and also the ability to drink until the sun coming up over Mayfair signals the need for a murderous training session. "I don't expect to live for ever," he says. But what life expectancy has he as a front rank force in English football? I think he will make it again and if I speak as one of the committed, as an admirer who has felt most the force of his personality rather than the sometimes raw and destructive edge of his ego, I can muster supporting evidence. At the same time I also have to recognise doubts.

Don Revie, the current England team manager, once said in a flash of anger following an Allison broadside, "That man Malcolm Allison is an embarrassment to the game." And Joe Mercer, his face drained, has declared to me, "I cannot imagine that anyone has a crueller tongue than Malcolm Allison." More recently I have heard it said by a man I tend to listen to that Allison is a "burned out case," that the trajectory of his violent, at times brilliant, career

7

has entered an irreversible decline.

There are, no doubt, grounds for some fears. But only, I believe, in the sense that Hemingway conveyed when he wrote: "If people bring so much courage to this world, the world has to kill them to break them, so of course it kills them." Allison's courage is not easily defined. It is not, particularly, of a physical kind. It is about an aggressive approach to life, the willingness to brave cross-fire to win a certain position.

Once, in the bar of a Portuguese train rattling up country to Coimbra, a stepping stone in Manchester City's march to the European Cup-Winners Cup in 1970, he explained his philosophy of life as it applied to football. I had asked whether he did not tire of the sometimes monotonous, possibly trivial, routine of the professional football man. He said to me: "A lot of people in football see the game as an end in itself. They do not relate it to life. They become dominated by it. It dwarfs them. I'll never be trapped by the game so that I am part of it once I have ceased to enjoy it. I love life and what I love about football is that you can compress into it all the strengths and the weaknesses of people. It is a mirror to life ... and there is much to see in it. There's courage, there's weakness, real fear. You can see boys becoming men in front of your eyes. You can see characters stretching, and dwindling."

If Malcolm Allison's character was ever to dwindle I suspect it would have happened in the last three years. His loss of status has been dramatic. But he has rolled back the sneers with a simple statement of intent. "Succeeding again, and doing it right back from square one, has become the great challenge of my life. It will give me more satisfaction than I have ever had before."

It is a lonely battle which has invited some popular scorn—of which Allison is himself contemptuous—but also deep admiration. Rodney Marsh, one of the few truly inventive and original players in English football and whose signing by Allison caused great controversy in 1972, tells me: "When Malcolm Allison walked away from Maine Road I felt a great emptiness. He has been the most important influence in my life. I know he will come through again because he is a big man, with big thoughts."

Frank McLintock, a distinguished player and one of the most experienced pros still practising his craft, is more open-minded, but he has this vision of Malcolm Allison: "I can see him living through incredible pressures, pressures which would knock out any other football men, and of him sitting at a table surrounded by friends, ordering champagne and not worrying about the bill, telling somebody exactly how you should prepare to smoke a good cigar. I suppose what I'm saying is that I think he is bigger than the game. Whatever happens to him in football there is an area in himself which he isn't going to expose to the business. There is a little bit of Malcolm which football can never get to."

Sometimes I have believed that there are impulses inside the man which he cannot himself get to. I know, for instance, that behind the stereotype of brash aggression is a man of considerable sensitivity, someone who delays the answer to a question for minutes, not out of indifference but out of a desire to give a reply of some precision. And I know too that for every night you might glimpse him sweeping into one of the West End's plushier watering holes, there are three when he retires to his Kensington flat with a book. And almost invariably it will either be biography or autobiography, and the quest will be to try to look inside the thoughts of big men.

There are aspects of Malcolm Allison which are not totally appealing. With rare exceptions, he prefers talking to listening, and there are times when you may struggle a little to define the point at which self confidence and arrogance become boorishness. Modesty does not sit easily on his broad shoulders. But then neither does hypocrisy or cant, or toleration of the stupid or the weak. He admits to certain coldness, to the point, in fact, of ruthlessness.

9

His behaviour at football grounds has often been less than dignified. Yet is that not balanced by the honesty of his reactions, and by his refusal to take cover under all the pressures he has experienced, for instance, at Crystal Palace? I have watched him closely over the last few years and rarely have I seen a man accepting more implicitly the reminder that Geoffrey Green, football's poet laureate, offers to the broken spirit of many a Soccer man: "Into every life a little rain must fall." Allison might fairly claim to have walked through a monsoon.

In that passage concerning the ravages that the world can inflict Hemingway also added: "The world breaks everyone and afterwards many are strong at the broken places." Such is my hope in the case of Malcolm Allison. For if he has been wild, foolish, perhaps even callous and unprincipled at times, he has never lost a certain basic strength. Nor, for me at least, the appeal of a man never afraid to say what he thinks or do what he feels needs to be done.

The colours of his life are painted in broad brush strokes. I believe it makes an interesting picture.

# *Prologue*

It is a rare and humbling thing to be invited to write an autobiography.

It tends to force you into corners of self criticism which in the normal way you would cheerfully avoid.

I have tried in these pages to give a true reflection of my life. And in doing so I have encountered much futility, much waste. But also I have come to the conclusion that every man's life must be of interest. It was a theory that filled me with scepticism at the start of the project.

Yet in re-tracing the years, the mistakes and the absurdities, I have been surprised at the number of lessons once learned and swiftly rejected.

Football is a peculiarly intense arena, in that it requires, at least once a week, a public examination of one's work. This can be a great stimulation, but it can also be the most demanding trial. I have tried to explain the effect such pressures can have on a man—and I have also tried to convey the feel and the colour of it.

There are a few peaks and quite a number of valleys in the contours of my life, and again I have tried to cover all the ground, explaining how each new situation affected me.

Of course some things have been left unsaid and perhaps

some will feel that others have been overstated, and certainly I believe that in such an effort of memory an element of self-justification is inevitable.

All I can say is that I have related my life as I have seen it and felt it. I have tried to acknowledge my mistakes, my selfishness, and I know there is much about my story which will not appeal to more conservative instincts.

But if I have regrets I also have some pride. I have lived my life the way I have wanted. I have not sat back to watch the world pass me by. I have gone out to fight for certain things. And at 47 years of age I have developed a new ambition—to live to at least 94. The ambition was prompted recently by the story of an old lady who went into a nursing home to die at the age of 92. She was given just a few days to live, and almost as her last act she decided she wanted to write a poem. She wrote a good poem and was so pleased with it that she decided she wanted to write more. That was two years ago. Her room is now filled with flowers. And she is still writing poems.

Her example inspires me to hope that this book is in the nature of a half-time report. And certainly I'm looking forward to the second half.

Malcolm Allison,
March, 1975.

# Chapter One

## The virgin soldier

All the sensations which have come to me in life, the bursts of success which have carried me away and those bitter moments of failure, have flowed from one simple conviction. It is that at the back of every man's mind there is a picture of the good life. It is his conception of what is right for him. It is his own, very individual goal. What is sad is that too often this can never be more than fantasy, a vulnerable hope which can only be fulfilled by a random piece of luck, like winning a treble chance on the football pools.

If my life is of any interest it may be because I have been able to live out my fantasies. The flesh of reality has come to them. I have stood, for instance, on the balcony of a hotel in Vienna watching the dawn break over the city after my team had won a major European Soccer trophy in the famous Prater Stadium ... a place I had looked at with awe as an 18-year-old national serviceman. I have walked into the old champagne bar at Royal Ascot, produced a roll of £10 notes and ordered 'drinks all round.'

Twice I have watched a team who I believed had become an extension of myself win brilliantly at Wembley, another great stadium which had caught my breath as a youngster.

And just weeks after the first Cup final win I found myself being fêted in Italy by one of the most powerful men in Europe, the Fiat magnate Agnelli. He said to me: "Come to coach my team Juventus, Malcolm, and I will pay you £20,000-a-year tax free and give you your own private aeroplane."

These are things which may not dazzle you. But they were important to me. I tell them to explain myself, my motives.

These motives are quite simple. I want to be a winner, a success, and I am prepared to follow this impulse as long as I believe I have something to put into life. I am known as a playboy and it is an image I cannot really argue about. My picture has been taken in too many nightclubs, with too many girls, too many bottles of champagne, for that. It is true that a beautiful girl, a bottle of good champagne, and a smooth Havana cigar are my idea of the basic ingredients for an enjoyable evening. But not necessarily so. And beyond that I have become aware that the only true, deep-down enjoyment flows from a sense of achievement, a feeling, when you sip your champagne or down your pint, that you have something to celebrate.

If you cannot feel that you deserve to celebrate, that you have brought a little effort, a little courage, to your day, then you might as well be drinking water, and that girl can quickly lose her charm. When I ran a club off Tin Pan Alley I saw too clearly that terribly sharp dividing line between enjoying yourself and merely seeking to submerge your failures, your fears, and perhaps a growing boredom with life. I once helped a rich customer out of my club. He was quite drunk. He had no control over himself. He had become a clown. I have never forgotten the thought that came into my head: "So this is being a playboy?"

I realised then that boredom with life was the ultimate failure. That you go through such phases is inevitable. I have had many. Grey mornings when you lay in your bed and asked yourself "What can I bring to this day. What have I got left in me?" I have seen many strong, talented men shrink in this way. They have let themselves stand still. They have lost the rhythm which made them what they were.

Football, in that it is the world into which I have put most of my hopes, my energy, and my thinking, has usually dictated my moods. But there have been other factors. I have gambled heavily, sometimes profitably, quite often badly. I have coached football at Cambridge University, and learned much from that.

There are things about my life of which I am not proud. I do not expect approval of the fact that I have had a good wife and fine children and that much of my time has been spent apart from them. I know that I have been ruthless, selfish, and at times possibly absurd. I cannot justify any of this. All I can say is that I have never run away from problems, that I have never pretended feelings or emotions which have not been there. It has caused the breakdown of my marriage. It has made me many enemies. But I do like to think of myself as a man who is honest, a man prepared to say, "This is me, all of me—I'm not holding anything back."

I also know that I have never lost an awareness of what life can be, of what rewards it offers a man ready to go the distance with all the wit, the strength, and the courage he can command.

Such an awareness can grow in you over the years—or it can come to you very suddenly. It came to me out of a clear blue sky above the Italian alps. I was an 18-year-old private soldier competing in the army ski championships at Cortina. We had gone up to Cortina by train from Graz, Austria. I had £200 in my pocket. I had been stationed in the Vienna of Harry Lime and for a young soldier who had his wits about him, didn't smoke, and got on well with a quarter-master obsessed with football, there were rich pickings in the black market.

I shall never forget that first drive through Cortina. The

great cities of Europe were shot to pieces, the ruling currency was cigarettes and penicillin, but here in the mountains life dazzled like the sun playing on the ski slopes. We passed brightly lit wine bars, shops filled with jewellery and watches, and in the cafés you could see beautiful girls clad in fur coats. All this set against those cold, magnificent mountains streaked with vivid colour.

I had £200 in my pocket and I felt poor. But also I felt for the first time what life could be. My most formative years had been spent in war-time London. Drab, grey days filled with ration books and demob overcoats. And now I found myself in a sort of capitalist Shangri-la. I found myself gawping at the shops, the girls. We stayed for two weeks. I spent all my money, reselling a watch for a fraction of the price I had paid. I couldn't get near those beautiful girls in the fur coats. They looked, one or two seemed as if they might be interested, but in Cortina, even in 1946, £200 was no base on which to attack café society.

But I looked, I absorbed the pattern of these extraordinary life styles, and the feeling came to me very strongly that I could never be content with an ordinary life. I had to have all this colour, all this exhilaration for myself.

With that exhilaration, as sharp and as clear as the mountain air, came a sense of identity, a sort of dawning feeling that I could begin to recognise myself. I had begun to see clearly what I wanted for myself. One thing was a sense of excitement, a heightened awareness of being alive, and this came to me dramatically on the Olympic ski slope.

We had finished our work one afternoon and the ski instructor was emphatic that the cable car was making its last run to the foot of the mountain. I had either to leave now or tackle the Olympic run, for which I had no adequate preparation. But the sun was still bright, I felt so good, and it seemed to me, over hot chocolate and a glass of brandy, that the beautiful girls might just be thawing. I lingered over my drinks, but not because of second thoughts or sudden fears. I wanted to savour that special excitement which comes to you when you know you are going to do something new and dangerous.

Looking out over the vast mountains and into the valleys, where hamlets stood out as no more than clusters of specks, it was easy to get a sensation of absolute detachment. Finally, I pushed gently into the run. For half a mile I journeyed into a private world, broken only by the rasp of my breath and the crackle of the skis. In one flash, though, the breath was out of my body. I had swept into a huge-sided tunnel.

Half way through this crude gash in the mountain there was a wicked bend. I tried to take it but I knew that there was no chance. I found myself sailing through the air, as though disembodied. That I did not break every bone in my body as I crunched into the snow was one of my first great pieces of good fortune. But I suffered a painful downpayment on that act of arrogance. For days my body ached and throbbed and on the train back to Graz the lads repeatedly asked: "Were you scared, what was the sensation?" I said it had been an "interesting experience." I didn't tell of the fear that comes in that sudden moment when you realise you may have possibly fatally misjudged, when you feel suspended between life and death. But if I had I wouldn't have been telling the whole truth. I also knew that I had done something important to myself.

For the first time I had done something after dismissing the consequences. And that, I realised, was a significant thing. I had done something out of the ordinary and I sensed that I may well have set a pattern for myself.

Those days in the army were important to me because they gave me a rough but colourful education. My schooldays, affected by war-time evacuations, had been sketchy as legally possible. My father was an electrician and I was always proud of our semi-detached house in Bexleyheath. I imagine it was an average sort of upbringing.

My outstanding achievement as a child was to win the

Victor Ludoram trophy at the local junior school. But I'm afraid it was the most hollow success. I tripped my closest rival in a vital race and in my defence I can only recall the shame I felt when the headmaster presented me with the trophy.

Football dominated all my thoughts. My teachers and my parents gave me up to that. I did work briefly for a Fleet Street photographic agency as a messenger boy but my clear recollection from those days was of having to leave Wembley Stadium just a few minutes into a Cup final. I thought the photographer was mad when he handed me some plates and told me to get them back to the office for developing. "But I want to see the match," I insisted. He roared at me to leave. I think that may well have been the most bitter moment of my life.

I joined Charlton Athletic as an apprentice professional but almost instantly the army claimed me. I joined up at Maidstone on a misty day in December, 1945. The army did ease my obsession with football. Though I never lost my ambition to make the game my life, the army did teach me that football was no more than an aspect, perhaps a reflection, of the hard business of life.

Just how hard the business could be was revealed to me in Austria. Two incidents, one dramatic, the other trivial, got through to me with particular force.

At one stage I was stationed at Klagenfurt, near a massive transit camp for refugees. It seemed to be a clearing house of despair. There were Czechs, Ukrainians, Russians, all gathered together in grey rows of Nissen huts. Often we drove past the camp and always the experience affected my mood for hours afterwards. These people shuffled and mooched, they didn't walk like ordinary men and women. Nothing about them suggested a shred of optimism. Never did I see from them an uplift of the shoulders, a posture that was other than beaten, weighed down by a great weight of bad experience.

Once we drove past in a heavy truck. It was dusk and the

camp looked even more desolate than usual. In a narrow lane we came to a woman carrying a baby in her arms. Without warning she threw herself and the child under the truck. They were both tossed aside, the baby disappearing in a slow arc over a hedge. They both had terrible injuries. We put them in a car which had stopped at the scene. We drove away in silence. No one had anything to say. I never learned their fate. That night I couldn't stop wondering what had been going through that woman's mind as she performed her act of desperation.

One afternoon a few days later I returned to my billet to find an orderly removing cigarettes from a drawer beside my bed. He didn't say anything, he didn't even seem startled by my arrival. He just stood there, his face totally without expression. Nothing that I might have said or done would have touched that man. He was living in his own, crushed world.

I am not suggesting that I dwelt on these incidents. They were, after all, no more than fleeting episodes in a great wave of new experience. But the sadness, the despair of those people did register with me. They come back to me, those people who had lost everything, including the will to live, when I see, for instance, rival football managers sweating with tension on a cold winter's night. I see a man, of great prestige, squirming in his seat and I ask myself: "How can grown men bring so much fear to a game of football?"

I am not talking, now, about a hatred of losing. I have always had that. I have seen football as an arena into which I can pitch in all my intelligence and my courage. And if my team is beaten I am also defeated. I have raged at referees I have considered instrumental in my defeat. I have been so disappointed at a result that I set out to get drunk. And in the morning it has been only with difficulty that I have traced my steps of the night before. Sometimes even that has been impossible. But I have allowed my tensions to well out of me. I never let them grow and fester within me.

Nor have I been so strangled by fears and doubts that I have been unable, say, to meet a group of football writers after a game.

Some managers look for the back door of a stadium. Frank O'Farrell, a close friend of mine, was for a time thrown completely by the pressures of his job as a manager of Manchester United. He began to feel that the press were determined to get him out. He began to retreat far inside himself. I remember ringing him up one day and inviting him to lunch. I thought I might be able to break some of the pressure building up inside him. He arrived in dark glasses and the first thing he said to me was: "Mal, you've brought me to a very busy place." I said, "Frank, it's a very funny thing about restaurants, they tend to get busy at lunch-times."

O'Farrell happens to be a man of great character, with a lot of integrity, and I only relate this incident to point out how hard it sometimes can be to keep a sense of proportion in a game which is caught halfway between sport and a desperate, neurotic business. Wilf McGuinness, O'Farrell's equally harassed predecessor at Manchester United, was once physically sick after a match with my team, Manchester City. And United won by three goals.

They were honest men attempting to do jobs under enormous pressure. I have faced similar pressures over the last two years at Crystal Palace. My reputation as a top Soccer man in this country has been on the line. But it has been a controlled worry—even when I have abandoned hopes of getting to sleep and walked around my flat in the small hours.

In this time I have had four opportunities to leave Crystal Palace. I have been offered national coaching jobs in Australia and Iran, a job in Vancouver, and my old club Manchester City asked me to go back. But I have seen a great challenge in this south London football club, which draws freakish crowds from the colourless suburbs. I have seen a chance to stand and fight the pressures and problems which have slaughtered so many of my colleagues in football management.

I have known managers who slipped away to their offices to down a couple of large scotches so that they could bear to watch the rest of the game. This, I know now, could never be my way. And for this I do owe a debt to those early insights in Austria. Those haunted, broken people in that camp of misery at Klagenfurt did teach me that in the matter of losing there are many degrees—and it is a lesson I have never forgotten.

In Vienna I learned of the sweeter side of life with a girl called Heidi. She was a blonde, lovely girl. I met her at a fair in the Vienna woods and we spent the day together. It was a day of many discoveries and when the time came for us to part, in a little square near the apartment block where she lived, I was delighted to see that she was not anxious to leave me. Eventually I gathered up all my nerve and said: "We have to make a big decision. I have to leave now—or you have to take me home." She took me home.

To get to her room I had to pass the place where her father slept. He was a 17-stone butcher. I crept past the foot of his bed, my army boots hanging round my neck. I never knew what reassurance could come with the sound of a snore. Nor the feeling of pride a young man carries with him from the bed of a supple young girl and on to the early-morning streets of a great city.

Not all my army experiences were so triumphant. Once I was lucky to escape the glasshouse. The incident, which could easily have become an international one in those hair-trigger days, occurred on a post in the mountains near the Yugoslav border.

It was an absurd business. My chief duty was to guard a Liverpool man called McCarthy, who had killed a Russian soldier in Vienna. Apparently he had got violently drunk and wandered into the Red sector. His first act was to attempt to climb a statue. When the unlucky Russian attempted to arrest McCarthy he was lifted off his feet and thrown over a bridge spanning the Danube. I found McCarthy a quiet, easy-going fellow and one break in the monotony was to take him for a walk along a mountain track. Our rations were poor and boring and we had become increasingly tempted by some chickens in a run beside a stone cottage. One late afternoon we cracked. I raised my rifle and fired at a chicken—and missed. Ridiculously, I repeated the process. McCarthy said: "For God's sake give me the gun." He grabbed a chicken and hit it with a rifle butt. We raced away, straight into the path of two Yugoslav border guards. They had their guns cocked. McCarthy again took my rifle, pointing it straight at one of the Slavs. They ran off.

That evening we sat around the cookhouse oven savouring the odours of roasting chicken. Until a full colonel of the Yugoslav army swung open the door and claimed his countryman's chicken. He drove away in his staff car, the chicken steaming beside him on the back seat. I suppose I was lucky to escape with a week's fatigues.

For all the army experiences, the ski-ing, the black market, the girls, there was one corner of me that was untouched. That was the footballer. I used to get out on the parade ground at five in the morning, going through training routines, building my strength.

One morning the C.O., taking a dawn gallop, was intrigued and impressed by my early training. So impressed, in fact, that the rest of the camp were ordered to get up an hour early for a course of P.T. It took me some time to recover from the unpopularity which came with that decision. I was asked to organise the battallion team and as an extra incentive to win the Regimental Cup I prepared a betting coup. The HQ team had several useful pros in their team and it was almost impossible to get a bet on them. We jogged through the early rounds and on the day of the final we were able to back ourselves nicely 7-1. We won 6-2.

More seriously, I used to watch the young Austrian footballers training at the Prater. I was deeply impressed. I liked the way they enslaved the ball. They made it do all the work. They were neat and controlled. There was nothing crude or haphazard about their work and I thought to myself: " 'surely this is the wave of the future. This is what we have to do in England!' " I was determined to take this thinking back to Charlton. I felt growing excitement as my demob date approached. I was going to put myself in the hands of top professionals, learn from them and try to adapt some of the ideas I had picked up from watching the Austrians.

But of all the things the army had taught me, there was still a blank in my education. I had not learned a healthy mistrust of some people's motives. But that was an omission professional football was swiftly to remedy.

# Chapter Two

## The player

Before I went into the army, to learn some things about myself and other people, the centre of my world was the Valley, the vast, scruffy bowl of concrete which is the home of Charlton Athletic Football Club. It is set in grey streets in the great sprawl of south-east London. But I could not have imagined a more romantic place. It was inhabited by giants.

At a newsagent's shop near the ground I used to buy the Evening Standard, the News, and the Star and pour over the small print seeking the name M. Allison in the lists of junior teams. I can still remember the sensation when I first saw my name in print and linked with a famous football club. It filled my whole body with a sense of pride and achievement. It is a feeling I try to recall when a young footballer, perhaps sullen and rebellious through a sense of injustice, comes to my office to talk over his problems. I find it easy to put myself into that youngster's skin. If I was so affected by the mere sight of my name in print, or its absence, it is not difficult to imagine how problems and reverses can magnify themselves in a young mind.

Most of all I recall the self-doubt which used to come to me when I began to measure myself against the established players. Then the optimism and the day-dreaming used to end. Instead, there was a feeling of almost impossible challenge. That feeling came to me most acutely when I played my first League match, as a 21-year-old, at Manchester City.

But by then optimism had been overtaken by a darker mood. I had become disgusted with the state of, and the thinking in, the game which I believed would shape my life. My determination to succeed had become desperate, but it was still my only motivation. And I knew now exactly how much I had to do for myself. I had discovered that in football, like almost every walk of life, there were not too many people eager to smooth the way for youthful ambition.

I have already recalled the impression made on me by the Austrian footballers at the Prater stadium, the thrilling sense of purpose and knowledge displayed by their trainers. I had been excited by the variety of their routines and their emphasis on mastering ball control. The contrast at Charlton Athletic, a club which had become a power in the land with their move from the old Third Division South to the First Division, was appalling.

It was like getting into a time machine and finding yourself travelling in the wrong direction.

What made things even more depressing was the fact that Charlton's trainer then was Jimmy Trotter, who also did the job for England. Trotter impressed me as a man—and as a physiotherapist. He was straight and honest and his treatment of injuries was swift and competent. But he betrayed a great ignorance of training methods. It seemed to me that he could never have given a moment's thought to the need for developing new ideas about the preparation of a professional footballer.

We were asked to jog aimlessly around the training ground. You could see boredom on every face. Training gear was ragged. It reflected the lack of thought behind our work. This may sound like the arrogance of a young man.

25

But I felt this very strongly, and all my experience since then has confirmed my earlier viewpoint.

I used to argue with Trotter and senior players like Bert Johnson and George Smith, who went on to manage several League Clubs. I knew they had dismissed me as an upstart, a young know-all. I recall Trotter asking me sarcastically, and in front of a group of senior players, "Come on Allison, what have you got to tell us today? You always have something to say." There were titters. I was still 20 and yet to make the first team.

In fact my position was weak—and very frustrating. For along with my disgust at the training régime of Charlton, I was aware of my own deficiencies as a player. I had clear ideas about what I wanted to do, but I knew I lacked pace. There were many parts of my game I had to improve, but there was nowhere to go for help.

When I played that first League game, at Maine Road, Manchester, at Christmas 1949, it was the first time in my life that I had felt truly alone and helpless. I cannot recall the flow of the game. But I recall vividly my state of mind that afternoon. I knew I was inadequately prepared for the biggest challenge of my life. This deficiency was at two levels. Physically I felt weak. We faced three games in four days over the holiday period and in that first match I knew I was spent.

In my ignorance I had burned myself out on the training pitch. My strength should have been growing a little with each of those games, but instead I was shattered after the first. Mentally, I was in a fog. There was no communication between the bench and the field. I think it was then that I realised for the first time that my chief satisfaction from the game might well come from coaching, from orchestrating the work of eleven men, of making those individuals into a smooth, coherent unit. It seemed like madness, in this ultimate team game, to send out men with no clear idea of how they related to each other once the referee blew his whistle.

Of course, much of football is instinct and natural talent. But these are qualities which should be harnessed and disciplined. The problem, in fact, was quite basic. Trainers did not occupy their jobs because of some inherent flair or feeling for the task. They were ex-players tied to the game because it was the only life they knew. It was a congenial, undemanding way to earn their living.

Always I had this feeling of disappointment about the people who were in charge of my career. No one seemed prepared to question what we were doing. In 1950 England was knocked out of the World Cup in Brazil by a team of amateurs representing the United States. But the shock waves from that result were easily absorbed by the dim, bland men whose voices were most powerful in English football. A pattern of play had been laid down by the great Herbert Chapman of Arsenal, and it had been untouched for nearly 20 years.

Fortunately, the Hungarians arrived from another planet in 1953. I went down to Wembley with Jimmy Andrews, later manager of Cardiff City. We got to the stadium early and watched the Hungarians working out on a patch of grass where they kept greyhounds. I noticed their light, modern gear and their streamlined boots and that registered with me vaguely. But Jimmy pointed out the 'pot' bulging from the red shirt of no. 10, Ferenc Puskas. "God, we'll murder this lot," he said. You had to agree, even though there was a neatness and skill about their limbering. Then, out on the pitch just before the kick off, I saw the 'fat guy' volleying shots into the arms of goalkeeper Grocis from 40 yards. I said to Jimmy, "They've got some skill, you know it could be interesting."

It was more than that. There was something so bright, so brilliant, in Hungary's 6-3 win that even the walls of complacency in English football began to crumble. There was no way that the revolution could come overnight. But what it did mean was that brave voices—like that of the most under-rated Walter Winterbottom whose thinking so far outstripped his actual performance as England manager—at least began to be heard.

I recall two examples of poor communication which affected me deeply at Charlton Athletic. Both concern Jimmy Seed, a man of vast prestige in the game. He had led Charlton into the First Division, and he had exploited a rich vein of South African talent—men like Eddie Firmani, John Hewie, and Syd O'Linn. But to me he didn't even grasp the essentials of his job. In three years at the club I had felt not one moment of real contact with him. He was a distant, uninvolved figure.

When the first team centre half Harold Phipps went down injured I assumed I would get my chance in the first team at the week-end. Nobody spoke to me about this, but it was a fair assumption. Then they posted the teams for mid-week games and I found myself in the third side. This seemed like complete humiliation. I had been playing well, knocking hard on the door. I went mad. The third team was at Brentford and I went down there in an enormous sulk. If someone had said: "Malcolm, we're playing you in the third team and having a look at you with Saturday's First Division match in mind", I would have played out of my skin. But instead I felt crushed, discarded. Mere conversation was missing.

On another occasion Charlton were playing a London Select team and our centre half Phipps was picked for that side. I came into the Charlton side to mark the England centre forward, Roy Bentley. I played him well, and after that game Seed came to me and said: "Son, you're just the centre half I've been looking for." I had been with the club five years.

My feelings of resentment towards Seed and the sort of man-management he had come to represent in my mind came to a head one afternoon at the Valley. I was training on my own; jogging around the track (what else?). Seed was showing an official of the South African FA around the ground. As I passed them Seed shouted: "That's it son,

28

lengthen your stride, that's what I want from you." I just ran by, completely ignoring him. He hadn't spoken to me for years but because there was somebody around he wanted to impress upon him that he was playing the big father-figure. I thought to myself: "Up you, the famous Jimmy Seed." I was completely disillusioned with the man. He called me into his office the following day and said: "When I speak to you I expect a reply." This was somebody who walked past you in a corridor as though you didn't exist.

About that time I met and came under the doubtful influence of Tommy Brown. He made an impression on me for a variety of reasons, and even at the time I realised they were not all good ones. He had style, a certain nonchalance, and he was the only man in the place who didn't adopt a servile attitude towards Jimmy Seed. He had reasons, though, to be sure of himself. He had played for Scotland at 17 and when Charlton bought him from Millwall he cost £7,000, a formidable figure in those days. He was a smart dresser, favouring well-tailored corduroy suits. Brown took me on my first night out in the West End.

I remember saying to him: "Tommy, you are so good, you have so much talent. You are always shirking training, looking for the easy way out." His reaction was one of amusement. "What's the point? I never bother until they start thinking of the retained lists in March and April."

In fact Brown was born some 20 years ahead of his time. He reacted fiercely against the fact that professional footballers were treated like cattle. His natural age would have been the one of Rodney Marsh, George Best, and Francis Lee, when rewards offered to star footballers are in keeping with their drawing power. In my youth and idealism I could not recognise or appreciate Brown's attitude. But I see it vividly now. Tommy Brown was reacting against the fact that he could perform his skills before vast crowds—and those were the days when locked gates were commonplace—and then travel home by bus.

Footballers were naively happy to be earning their living in a way that pleased them. They didn't think in terms of exploitation and serfdom, of a system which enabled a club to hire 60 professionals because wages were so low.

When I was transferred from Charlton Athletic to West Ham I led myself to hope that the futility and the bitterness was over.

For a while I was happier, but it was merely the change of environment which had broken the monotony. Within six months I was more disillusioned than ever. Not only did West Ham know less about training than Charlton, a feat which I would have believed impossible, but they asked for less effort. The only difference in the training sessions were that West Ham's were shorter. The facilities were disgraceful. We used to train on a pockmarked, scruffy little track at the back of the ground. We used to have to run in and out of a copse of trees. It was impossible for the trainer to keep his eyes on all the players. If he was alert he might spot blue cigarette smoke filtering through the trees.

My relationship with the West Ham manager Ted Fenton was much closer than the one I had had with Jimmy Seed. But it was scarcely satisfactory. I did give him some problems, but they arose chiefly out of my frustration with the way the club was run. And eventually I began to run the team, with his tacit agreement. He could see that I was getting results. Player power is a phrase which has become fashionable in modern football. But it was being practiced in the West Ham dressing room 20 years ago. I began to draw up my own training schedules, and people like Phil Woosnam, Noel Cantwell, John Bond and Frank O'Farrell came in with me.

Looking back I'm amazed at how one-dimensional I was in those days. My dedication was absolute. I didn't smoke, I didn't drink, and I never had sex within three days of a match. Incredible! I became the first player in England to wear short shorts. The reason was simple. I felt it was time for a change. The Continentals had brought in lighter gear and I got hold of some lightweight South American boots. Ted Fenton was invited to become Adidas agent in Britain. He laughed at them: "England's footballers will never wear these slippers," he said. It was this fixed, stonewall attitude that made me very bitter.

West Ham had put me into a club house in Barkingside, near Ilford. It was a small, pleasant house in a terrace. The rent, which was to be paid into an estate agent's office opposite the West Ham ground, was 30 shillings a week. One lunch-time after training, Fenton called me into his office. He said: "Malcolm, you owe 75 weeks' rent. What are you going to do about it?" I replied: "What are you worrying about? I'm playing well, aren't I?" He went white. "Do you want to transfer me?" I asked.

Nothing mattered to me except the way things were going out on the field. Playing the game was always such a joy to me because it gave me absolute release. I can recall the feeling I used to get when the referee started the game. I might be weighed down by debts, bookmakers might be looking for me, but once the game started I used to think: "No one can touch me now. This is my island." It was a terrific feeling.

Once I got kicked in the chest at Sheffield Wednesday and I collapsed. I couldn't get any breath and I thought, "This is it, I'm dying." One thought came into my head. "I've got £200 in my pocket in the dressing room. £200 unspent." After my dressing down by Fenton over the rent arrears I went to West Ham dogs. And won £360. I paid off the arrears the following morning.

The very fact that West Ham was a loosely organised club gave me my chance to make a mark. At that time I was going off to coaching courses at the Lilleshall centre. I met people like Winterbottom, Alan Brown, and Arthur Rowe. In their different ways they all impressed me. And in that atmosphere I sensed that I could make an impact. My knowledge was limited, my ideas half-formed, if that, but each time I returned to Upton Park with a new enthusiasm.

I was able to bring some variety to our training. And Fenton allowed me to get on with it.

We had some good players, people like Vic Keeble, Johnnie Dick and Cantwell, and because we were all good friends we were able to talk and argue long into the night after visits to the Hackney dog track. In a café around the corner from Upton Park we used to fill the room with our theories and disputes. But the result was that we were a nicely developing team. We had opened our minds and declared ourselves willing to try new things and be prepared to make some mistakes on the way. In 1956 and '57 we were emerging as certainties to eventually find our way to the First Division.

We had moved, in terms of tactical sophistication, a long way from the night in 1953 when AC Milan appeared in a friendly match at Upton Park. They beat us 6-0. They had five internationals of different nationalities in their forward line. Ken Brown was centre half for us, I was at left half. When Gunnar Nordhal appeared in the centre circle Ken Brown turned to me and said, "Oh God, what a bloody giant." He stood 6 ft. 3 inches, weighing 15-stone. And he was a magnificent player. They also had the great South American Schiaffano. We all struggled. They were all so much more accomplished in ever phase of the game. They worked brilliantly off the ball and all their players could beat a man when they needed to. I remember getting on the trolley bus to go home, feeling very low. A chap got on the bus complaining about the team, all the way to Ilford. It was a painful journey.

Apart from the diversion of dog and race track, I found my life centring almost entirely around Upton Park. We used to train in the morning and most afternoons I would stay behind to take some coaching, often with Cantwell and Bond.

Fenton used to pay me £3 extra for training the schoolboys at night. It was then that I found I had a bit of a gift for spotting the boys most likely to make it as

32

professionals. There is one classic example. One intake of youngsters at Upton Park included Bobby Moore—and a boy called Georgie Fenn. Bobby looked a useful prospect. Fenn was considered a certainty to make a really spectacular name for himself. All the big London clubs had gone for him, but he came from an East End family and he chose West Ham. Georgie had scored nine goals in one match for England boys, and he was also an English schools sprint champion.

After a fortnight of training the boys Fenton called me into his office to ask my opinion of the intake. I said I liked this boy and that, and when I finished he said: "But what about Georgie Fenn?" I said that I didn't give him much of a chance. I didn't like his attitude, he wasn't interested enough. There didn't seem much of a commitment. Fenton threw up his arms and said: "But the kid has so much talent." I said it was a pity but I just couldn't see the Fenn boy making it. At the same time I said that Bobby Moore was going to be a very big player indeed. Everything about his approach was right. He was ready to listen. You could see that already he was seeking perfection.

Down the years George Fenn has written to me twice, once saying that he was planning to make a come-back. But he never played seriously after drifting away from West Ham. It was a tragedy, as sad in its way as the early retirement of that other Georgie, Best. Fenn could have been just as big as Best. He had sensational speed, all sorts of trickery, and a tremendous shot. But however hard you tried with him you had a sense that it was all futile. Something inside him sent out the strong message: "I don't really want to know." Deep down, perhaps it was the drudgery of training and the battle for constant fitness that put him off.

Certainly the life of a professional footballer is incredibly monotonous in its repetition. Yet when I look back I can only remember my love for the endless circle of training, playing, getting treatment, and then training again. I used

33

to get up in the morning and feel like singing. And then, when it was over and I had suddenly become very ill, I felt numb for more than a year. My attitude to people, everyone, my wife, my family, my friends, hardened.

If I am very honest I will admit that I still feel bitter about the way my playing career ended so swiftly, and so short of fulfilment. It is a hard thing to feel that life has cheated you out of the one thing that had seemed to make it worth living. But I do know that I was a limited footballer. I knew I was useful, but I could never relax on what talent I had.

Yet I did have my ambitions as a player. At times I felt I was playing well enough to at least challenge for an England place, and this was especially so at the time Billy Wright was converted into a centre half and won his 'extra' caps.

The most memorable game I played in was a sixth round FA Cup tie at White Hart Lane. West Ham had knocked out Huddersfield, Blackburn, and Preston comfortably and we went to White Hart Lane in a good, composed mood. They locked the gates at the ground half an hour before kick off. It was a 3-3 draw, a marvellous game. We lost the replay at Upton Park.

In 1958 we were moving smoothly towards promotion to the First Division and I was playing at my peak. The 'player power' revolution I had put so much of my time into was an established fact—and manager Ted Fenton was not complaining. We had got ourselves into a winning run, we had begun to assume that victory was our right—and that is the most vital strength a football team can possess.

It was in a night match, at Sheffield United, that I suddenly realised I could no longer run. A Sheffield United player showed me the ball and then took it past me. I pumped my arms and struck out my legs, but there was no response. He just sailed away. It was an eerie experience. I managed not to panic. Substitutes were not allowed in those days and I eased myself through the game, conserving every possible scrap of energy.

I was able to disguise the situation. I had this feeling that it might just go away. But I was desperately worried. After the team returned to the hotel, I walked the streets of Sheffield in a daze. It was as though my life might just have ended. My room-mate Noel Cantwell was awakened by my heavy coughing in the small hours. With the coughing, which went on until morning, it was clear that something had gone wrong. And it was not as though I hadn't had warning. The previous Friday we had trained at Upton Park before leaving for a game in Bristol and I had found myself puffing and leg-weary. But the game had not brought a crisis. I told myself that I had run through the problem.

In fact I should never have played at either Bristol or Sheffield. I had had two bouts of Asian 'flu in three weeks. But stupidly I had pressed on. The team were playing well. I did not want to lose my place.

Cantwell went to see the manager in the morning after the Sheffield game and within days I was in The London Hospital, listening to a specialist saying, as though to someone else: "Mr. Allison, I think you have to forget about playing football. You have TB quite severely. We will have to remove one lung."

I didn't feel despair. I simply didn't accept what he was saying.

In that way I suppose I stepped outside of reality. It was only down the months that the bitterness grew. West Ham were going through to the championship and when I should have been collecting my first medal in football I was instead inhabiting a vast, grey void. Repeatedly I was advised to think in terms of a future which didn't include playing football. I tried to do this, but I found it impossible. I kept returning to the statement: "I can do it again. I have to." I couldn't get rid of the taste of bitterness when I left hospital. I went to West Ham's championship banquet at the Café Royal, and walked out when I learned that I was not to receive a championship medal. I had played six League games before my illness and the other players who had played the same number of games received medals.

This probably seems petty. Medals, in fact, do not mean that much to me. What got into me was the fact that West Ham were not prepared to recognise what I had done for the Club. But that, I'm afraid, is a familiar pattern in football. When I became ill, and the club had won promotion, Ted Fenton didn't want me around the place. Perhaps he saw me as a threat.

There was to be no recognition of my contribution off the field. I was reminded of this situation when Queen's Park Rangers sold Terry Venables to my club Crystal Palace last season. In football it was common knowledge that Venables had wielded vast influence amongst the players, that his contribution to the success of the team rivalled that of manager Gordon Jago. Yet Venables found himself sold without consultation. To me that was a depressingly familiar situation.

I did make a come-back attempt with West Ham. I suppose I knew that it was doomed, but I felt I owed it to myself to make the effort. I cannot say that I received much encouragement from West Ham officials, with whom I had several rows. But I'm prepared to accept that I cannot have been the easiest man in the world to deal with at that time.

I was playing quite well in the reserves, feeling my way gradually. Then, quite suddenly, it seemed that the door had swung open again. West Ham were due to meet Manchester United in a League game and we had had a few injuries. Endlessly I worked out the possible permutations that Fenton could make to his team. He decided that the choice for the number six shirt lay between Bobby Moore and me. That was ironic enough. Bobby, who remains a warm personal friend, had always tagged on to my heels. He was always asking me questions and I was glad to talk to this boy who deserved to make himself a great career. "But not yet, Bobby, not yet," I said to myself. The greatest irony of all was that Fenton called Noel Cantwell into his office and asked him, "Who should I play Allison, or Moore?" Noel had always been my right hand man at West Ham. We were the closest friends, our thoughts about the game and our attitude to life coincided at so many points. He said to Fenton: "I think you should play the kid."

That was the finish of Malcolm Allison, footballer.

For months afterwards I said to myself, "If only I could have played against United." I had worked it all out. I would have been marking Ernie Taylor, and though I wasn't really fit I could have got away with it. I was going to let him play in his own half. As it happened West Ham were well on top, and that would have suited me. I would have been able to play some nice long balls, to cruise through the game. It was a long time afterwards that I told Noel Cantwell how much his decision had hurt me.

My career with West Ham ran quickly to a close after Cantwell's honest—and in the circumstances of our close friendship, brave—decision. Bobby Moore was on his way and, in a different sense, so was I. I've often wondered what the effect of a late run in First Division football would have had on me. I imagine it may have untangled some of that confusion I felt when illness cut me down. It might have taken some of the intensity out of me. As it was I sensed that my presence was not exactly welcomed by the West Ham management. But, by the standards of those times, the club did treat me well financially. They organised a testimonial match and from that I received £3,000.

It was enough for me to buy the club house in Barkingside. But I couldn't get rid of the feeling that I had been harshly treated. A terraced house in an unfashionable suburb, though acceptable in other terms, had never been the sort of goal I had pursued in those nine years at West Ham. I had given everything I had to the club and I knew that I had done a lot to re-shape it, to prepare it for a new age of football.

In a sense, though, I suppose my ultimate frustration at

West Ham was set against the fact that the club had given me my head, allowed me to make my first strides in work which would later bring me so much success, particularly at Manchester City. It's also true that my illness had coloured all my thoughts. I did tend to feel that I had been caught in a great conspiracy to put me down.

Even so I could have made an immediate start to a coaching career. Spurs and Ajax offered me jobs. Bill Nicholson rang me to say I would be welcome on his coaching staff. And Ajax, on the recommendation of Ted Drake, offered me £34 a week to join them. I went to Amsterdam for four days and I liked what I saw. But for weeks I had been asking myself: "What am I going to do with my life now?" And I wasn't sure that I wanted to stay in football. I had given so much to my playing career and now it was over I couldn't see clearly into the future. For the first time in my life I was without a goal.

I felt that I needed time away from football. I had got too wrapped up in it. I felt I needed to try to see some more of life. So I went racing—for two years.

# Chapter Three

## Two years at the races

It was a long, uncertain journey from the dressing room of West Ham United to the champagne bar at Royal Ascot. I didn't lightly swap the world of football for that two-year sweep through the racetracks of Britain and France.

But there is a time, I imagine, in every man's life when he feels that deep inside him something has died. Perhaps it is the optimism, the reckless courage of youth which has slowly drained away. Maybe the spring has gone from his stride at that moment when he realises finally that all those ambitions and hopes he has stored away at the back of his mind can never be fulfilled. It is a process which can come to a man in a sudden storm of circumstances, or slowly down the years, nagging and wearing until at last the bleak point is made. Mine came like a stealthy thief, robbing me of the one thing which has brought me most pride and pleasure—my ability to play professional football at a high level.

Tuberculosis struck me hard and suddenly. One day, as far as I was concerned, my life was touching perfection, a rhythm of physical action and great fitness. The next I was broken, washed up into a situation which resembled a strange and hostile shore. It was such a cruel, random thing that it took me a long time to grasp its full meaning. For a while I simply refused to face the facts. When an eminent doctor told me I would never play again I shook my head slowly. And when, in long and very lonely nights in a sanatorium down in the Sussex countryside, I began to slowly accept that I might indeed be finished I had an urge to lash out. Great waves of depression rolled over me in those nine months at the sanatorium. At times I felt desperate, caged. I recall going to the chapel one Sunday evening. It was the first time I had gone to a church since boyhood and it was not so much a religious gesture as one of despair.

Religion is a subject I find difficult and disturbing. I was drawn to that little chapel by the feeling that I needed help from somewhere. I had been told that my progress had halted. There was no apparent reason. Simply, I had to face again a stage of my recovery which I thought had passed. I went to that chapel to ask: "What have I done to deserve this? How can a young man who has dedicated his life to being perfectly fit be cut down like this?" These were self-pitying questions, I know, but they were asked before I had had time to adjust my thoughts—and speak with people in a far more serious condition than myself.

The news that I was standing still came like an axe blow. When people like Noel Cantwell and Bobby Moore came down to see me I felt a strange gulf between us. Once the entire West Ham team arrived at the sanatorium. They were noisy and they tried hard to lift my spirits. But I could feel only embarrassment. Here were men with whom I had shared everything, the joy and elation of victories, the depression you carry with you from a defeat in some distant corner of the land. But now it was as though they had become strangers. They seemed as remote as the submarine commander who shared my room. He was so mean that he watched his television set with a headphone attachment; so tight inside that he wasn't even prepared to let the sound out of his set.

I suppose my desperation showed itself. One afternoon I slipped out of the sanatorium with another patient. This was strictly against the rules. I remember sitting in one of the village pubs, sipping a shandy, and feeling hunted. Each time the door opened I gave a start. The illness had not only taken away my fitness. It had put all sorts of doubts and confusion where before there was only an easy, simple confidence in myself.

Eventually I was allowed to distribute the newspapers around the sanatorium. That sounds like a trivial thing, but it proved to be very important. It meant that I was forced into the company of people who brought to their problems—which in one sense were similar to mine—so many different attitudes and levels of courage and resignation. I recall the actress Ursula Howells, a fine pleasant woman, coming to terms with her illness.

I was grateful to the man who finally broke my mood. He was an obviously wealthy business man, clad in a superb silk dressing gown. I got to talking with him one morning. We were talking generally but he must have detected my feelings. He must have seen the confusion on my face. He said to me: "Son, if ever your only problem is money you have no problems." I asked him what he meant. He explained that 18 months earlier his doctor had told him that he needed immediate treatment. He had told his doctor that there was no way that he could leave his business affairs. Though he had £80,000 in his personal bank account he had just got involved in a contract which ensured a quick £20,000.

Four days after our conversation the businessman was dead. It was one of those incidents, very clear in their implications, which can affect your thinking. Certainly it influenced mine. It took a lot of self-pity out of me. Here was a man who had been presented with the meaning and realities of life only on his death-bed. He had been given no chance to exploit his new knowledge.

At 29 I was in need of that sort of reminder of how easy it

41

is to lose your sense of proportion. I had allowed the prospect of my football career's ending to colour all my thoughts. Not for the first time in my life did I sense that perhaps I had reacted too strongly to a situation.

The worst of my crisis was over. But in place of that first horror there came uncertainty. Once my recovery was in sight I couldn't leave the sanatorium quickly enough. Yet no one could tell me how a professional athlete should adjust to the effects of tuberculosis. Not even the distinguished head of the sanatorium, Sir Geoffrey Todd. I had to feel my way. But I had made some strides forward. I was eager to get into the world again, whatever role I found for myself. I had had time to re-examine myself and I think it was this period which allowed some of the better aspects of my character to emerge. I looked at myself and saw a lot of impatience, arrogance, and perhaps a touch of ruthlessness. I felt some regret for the impatience and anger I had shown to older men—men for whom I had made clear my lack of respect. Perhaps I could now atone for some of that.

I awoke at dawn the morning I was due to leave the sanatorium. My bags were packed and I made hasty farewells. Noel Cantwell was driving down to take me home. He was late—by four hours. Right to the end it had been a long, hard year. On the drive up to London I sensed the frustrations which were to come with my attempted come-back as a West Ham player. At the back of my mind the question nagged: "If I fail, how am I to earn my living?"

After parting with West Ham I coached the amateur club Sutton briefly—and looked around, not knowing quite what I wanted to find.

I found it when I drove down to Epsom one afternoon. The Downs were bathed in sunshine and I was delighted to bump into an old friend, Arthur Shaw. Arthur is one of those men you can be very sure about, very quickly. I had got to know him in his days as a good, solid Arsenal defender. I think the gambling bug had got into him at about the age of nine. He greeted me in his usual open fashion. "Malcolm, I know a very good thing in the first race here tomorrow." I suppose business partnerships have been forged on a more casual basis than that, but there cannot have been many.

Arthur's proposal was that I should join him for a time in his life as a professional gambler. We got on well together, we knew how to make each other laugh, and the promise was one of making money and getting a bit of enjoyment out of life. It was a proposition which exactly suited my mood. I told him that I had some good information on one or two dogs running at West Ham that night. We agreed that the partnership should start immediately.

We made an excellent if modest start. Our winnings that first night at West Ham amounted to £150. But by the following evening, after Arthur's 'good thing' had strolled in comfortably, those winnings had swollen to £800. It was the opening flurry to a year in which I never knew what it was not to have a huge roll of notes in my pocket.

We didn't keep a ledger but I estimate that we must have won something in the region of £80,000 that first year. Of course I bought a few suits—and the notes seemed to burn through the expensive linings. Do I need to add that I bought a flash car? It was an American-styled Simca Cadet.

I got right away from football. My only contact was to take a few close friends like Cantwell and Noel Dwyer up to the West End. I watched a few matches, but I never allowed the game to exert its old pull on my thoughts and emotions. I pushed myself back into the world of racing. I suppose it was pure escapism, a sort of fantasy world where money lost all meaning. I could lose £2,000 and it had no more significance than seeing a threepenny bit fall through a grid.

It was then that I had my my first glimpse of the hollow centre of a playboy world. For I found myself trying to celebrate the winning of money. I tried hard enough.

43

Thousands of pounds went into the attempt. But all the time I knew, at the back of my mind, that this was a false thing. How can you truly celebrate a game of chance? Of course it is possible to congratulate yourself on good judgment, evidence that your nerve is holding. Arthur Shaw's knowledge, his shrewdness and his ability to immerse himself completely in this world earned my respect. He was doing something he truly loved. Here was a man who knew what he wanted out of life—and he had taken a lot of risks to go out after it. For me, I sensed almost from the start, it was something else. While Arthur was perfectly in tune with the business, relishing every aspect, I was floating on the surface.

It was an enjoyable experience, with moments of fleeting excitement, but there was never that feeling of deep satisfaction which had come to me during a game of football.

My greatest justification, in fact, was that I was spending my time with a warm friend, a man who had my complete trust and whose company was enjoyable and stimulating. We had a million laughs. When Arthur was down—it was a very occasional thing—I would buoy him up. He also had strict rules. He introduced me to one of them after our first day on a racecourse. We had lost £7,000. Nothing had gone right. The more we had tried to get out of trouble the worse it had got. We drove away from the track in complete silence. Arthur's face was grey, his forehead creased into a great frown. I thought to myself: "Oh dear, this is going to be a nice evening." Suddenly Arthur looked down at the dashboard and said: "Right, that's it—we're seven miles away from the track, that's the end of the gloom."

He had this feeling that once you were a certain distance away from a racecourse it was reasonable behaviour to forget the disasters of the day. He believed you had to serve a short, swift penance while you considered carefully your mistakes—and cursed your bad luck. Then it was legitimate to resume the business of looking with optimism towards another day's racing.

We pulled off the road into the forecourt of a lavish hotel, ordered a superb dinner and a couple of bottles of claret.

Inevitably Arthur was very much the senior partner. He nursed me along, conscious that we had different contributions to make. I used to bet with the bookies on the rails, trying to get good prices, possibly a point better than was going. I have always had a good eye for running power and Arthur would ask me to watch a specific horse in a race. He had a staggering number of contacts on the courses and my face was not completely unknown. Arthur used to study form, and cross-check with contacts on how certain horses had been going on the gallops, and I would try to keep my eyes and ears open.

Sometimes, I have to admit, there were some ludicrous results and occasionally we found ourselves talking a different language. Once in Baldoyle Arthur remarked: "the favourite is wearing heavy boots." A famous jockey was riding the horse and when he mounted I said to Arthur: "His boots don't seem that heavy, Arthur." He gave me a long, disbelieving look.

I recall one afternoon when we put £700 on a very likely prospect at Sandown Park. It had one serious rival, an animal owned by Charlie Chandler, who owns Walthamstow Stadium. Chandler walked into the ring to talk to his trainer and we watched their conversation very intently, hoping to get some indication of their feelings about the horse. Eventually Chandler left the paddock without a hint of his feelings. Arthur snapped: "Follow him, Malcolm, see what he backs." I pursued him through the trees and shrubs as he walked to the owners' and trainers' enclosure, where I expected him to go up to one of the big bookmakers to place his bet. But he strode past them. I looked around and saw Arthur waving me on, shouting: 'Keep on his heels, Mal." Chandler walked on into Tattersalls. I was now beginning to feel just a little self-conscious. Again he passed the bookmakers and walked on beyond the Tote. I was astonished to see him approach an ice cream van. That must mean the end of my assignment. But Arthur roared: "See what he gets, plain or choc ice!"

One of our good, early coups came at Ayr. We got strong information on a horse called Golden Disc. I saw the boxer Terry Spinks in the paddock and I told him to get on the horse. Later, I went down to the bookmaker with a sack and remember him muttering: "Bloody London burglars" as he filled it with fivers. I smiled and thought: "and those footballers are on £15 a week." Bringing off such a coup, such a nice, clean operation was the nearest thing to feeling true satisfaction. More often there were days when you wondered exactly what you were doing.

Such a day came at Hamilton Park. It was bleak and cold, just to emphasise the futility of our journey. We had gone to back just one horse, and we put down £800 to win £1,400. The owner was a bookmaker, and a fellow from the bookies' ring went into the paddock to talk with him. I was on scouting duty again. They had a very brief conversation and the man from the ring immediately walked out of the paddock, gave a brisk wave to the bookmakers indicating that the horse would not be trying. Desperately we settled on a saver, a 4-1 bet on a useful horse. That horse was left at the start. We had paid out £950 and got no more than a canter for our money. That's when everything goes wrong, when you get your first clear indication that ultimately there can only be one winner—the bookmaker. I think we drove a little more than seven miles that night before debating what we should eat for dinner.

In those two years I suppose I visited just about every racecourse in England and Scotland—and quite a few in Ireland. But the highlights of the year, apart from perhaps the Derby and Royal Ascot, were the weekend trips to

France, to Deauville and Longchamps. I was always dazzled by the style and grace of a French racecourse. And one weekend at Deauville still glitters brightly in my memory.

It started with an evening at the casino where Larry Geld, an American who sold half his business for 27 million dollars, bought £10,000 worth of chips and invited Arthur and myself to take a quarter share. We did—and watched it disappear in 20 minutes. The table was rope off like a boxing ring and I peered, fascinated, through the blue haze of cigar smoke. One hand was worth £30,000. Our man played for nine hours, fighting his way back into the game and finishing £3,000 up. I was very impressed—and even more so when he gave us our £2,500 back.

Gregory Peck was at the races. But I was more impressed with a young Rothschild lady. I cannot recall her Christian name, but I do remember her classic looks and elegant clothes. I had seen her at the casino, when most of my attention had been taken up by the card players, but at the races the following day I got into conversation with her. I asked her to dinner. She accepted promptly.

We ate very grandly and drank the best champagne. I remember thinking that whatever happened on the track the following afternoon it could still be said that I had made contact with real money. Of course I was enormously impressed. Dining with a Rothschild at Deauville struck me as good progress for the recently retired West Ham centre half.

Arthur was non-committal about my glory. He had information from the millionaire Larry Geld, who knew such things as the financial standing of a family like the Rothschilds. Eventually Arthur roared: "Trust you Malcolm—you find a Rothschild and she's skint."

The point of the weekend, in fact, was to back a Paddy Prendergast horse called Linacre. Paddy was friendly with Arthur and he had passed on firm information that his horse was in with an excellent chance. It had been moving beautifully on the gallops, and Prendergast had got the horse to France in perfect condition. The starting price was 40-1 and we had £600 worth. We stood to win £24,000. As the horses came under orders—with Linacre's price holding at 40-1—Prendergast couldn't contain himself any longer. He was surrounded by the richest backers on the track, including Larry Geld, and he said: "Look at my horse. It's going to win." It was a tape start and as Paddy was speaking one horse broke away snapping the tape. It was false start. It took them six minutes to get the horses away. Six minutes that seemed like hours. Geld and his friends sent people rushing to place heavy bets on Linacre. The price plummeted to 13-1. Of course Linacre ran superbly, finishing a comfortable winner.

We had lost £16,200 in six minutes. Yet my memory of that weekend remains one of exhilaration. It may have been still more escapism, but it was of a high order. There was colour, excitement, and if the girl was penniless it is still true that she was a beauty. No one could take that away.

Deauville represented the peak of my racing days. It was an explosion of colour; a time when, briefly, it did seem to me that there could be no other way to live. If that was the high, there can be no doubt about the low—a bitter squabble with Albert 'Italian' Dimes. Italian Albert won fame in his razor duel with the celebrated villian Jack 'Spot' Comer. He wasn't a bad lad really, but he did tend to trade on the notoriety that came with the Jack Spot incident. He owed me £300, which is not the sort of thing I would normally make a fuss about. But I knew that Albert was carrying a lot of money and I felt strongly that he should return my loan. He shrugged off my request—which made me very angry. I said to him: "Look you don't frighten me with your reputation. I'll fight you, straight up." To which Albert replied: "O.K. we'll fight, me and you straight up—with choppers". Albert meant axes! I never got the money.

The race gangs had broken up by this time, but there were always a few villains about. You knew something was

48

'on' when they got their heads together in a bar. It was quite amusing. I knew some of the men involved in the great gold bullion robbery, but only on a social level. It was not a world I wanted to get too closely involved with. What I could do was appreciate their sense of humour, and an intelligence that if channelled into legitimate business would have made many of them rich men.

I cannot recall precisely the moment I decided I had to walk away from the world of racing—and my great friend Arthur Shaw. It was a mood which grew on me steadily over a period of months. We had begun to lose money, and although we were still in the black I was getting an inkling of how hard it could be fighting out of a bad run. I began to see men who had been forced back into living on their wits. It seemed to me a terrible, desperate business. Win or lose, Arthur was committed to the life of a gambler. It had no such hold on me. I had enjoyed the freedom, the fresh air, the moments of incredible excitement. But I had never seen myself growing old in the game. I didn't relish a life-long battle with the bookmakers. In fact I would like to see bookies banned. They have always crucified the working man, in my opinion.

You do not think of such things when a good winner comes gliding home. All the disappointments, the grievances are wiped away. The day I bought champagne all round in the bar at Royal Ascot was a case in point. I walked into that bar feeling so content, so happy, I wanted to share the sensation. The barmen blinked when I made the order. But I wasn't interested in being the big man. I wasn't looking for reactions. It was simply an expression of the mood that came to me when my luck was running smoothly. But when that luck breaks, on a racecourse, you know you have a struggle on your hands. Your confidence begins to snap, you sense that the odds are beginning to rise against you.

It had all started in the sunshine at Epsom. And it finished in the rain at Kempton Park. We had another poor day and there was only the sound of the windscreen wipers as we drove away. Eventually I said: "That's it Arthur, I'm finished." He replied: "O.K. son, we've had some good times." I suppose we had covered about seven miles from Kempton Park.

# Chapter Four

## Christine Keeler and other lovers

I suppose Christine Keeler was a bit of a challenge to my ego. Here was the most infamous woman in the land, a girl whose ability to fascinate and enslave men had torn to pieces the morale of a Tory government. And I had heard in the Star pub in Belgravia—a place she visited regularly—that she had seen me on television and, shall we say, quite fancied me.

That is the sort of situation which always brings out the worst of my arrogance. I wanted to know and talk with this woman who had caused so much havoc, inspired so many sensational headlines. And perhaps make love to her.

Our first date was at the Guinea, the famous steak restaurant in Bruton Square. She had dyed her hair blonde, but she remained instantly recognisable. There was still much of the tigress in her. I was astonished by the reaction of the other men in the restaurant. She drew them like a magnet. A waiter dropped a plate.

I found her a strong and interesting woman. We went out, in fact, a couple of times. I recall that we made love.

Maybe she suspected that really I was involved no more than a piece of bravado. Certainly it was a relationship destined to be brief. It had no sounder foundation than a flickering television image and an incredible, monster reputation. I recall that we made love.

I take no pride in any of this. The whole affair was over almost before it began. My reaction to the whole situation, I suppose, was the one of the male mind working at its lowest level. I mean the business of pursuing a woman simply out of a need to prove something, however fleeting.

As it happened, Christine Keeler proved to be a formidable woman—and she obviously knew quite a bit about the male mind. For both of us this was no more than a diversion along the way. In fact I have never glorified sex for its own sake, despite the implications of that pursuit of Christine Keeler. Millions of men may have fantasised about the sexual prowess of this girl ... and millions more may have been repelled by her way of life, by the destruction and despair in which she found herself.

If I am honest I will say that her appeal to me stemmed almost entirely from her notoriety, the feeling that this girl—this call girl—was clearly out of the ordinary. I wanted to know what it was about her that could bring a powerful government trembling to its knees, that could trigger a scandal which brought anxiety and fear racing through Westminster and Mayfair like a chill wind. How was it that one young woman could bring such a cloud across so many successful and apparently well ordered lives? The answer was, of course, absurdly simple.

She was a very sexy woman.

That is the one clear impression I took away from our brief affair. The small talk and the laughter which accompanied the champagne and the haute cuisine fade against that central fact. But, looking back, it seems strange to me that I was involved, however briefly, with the girl. She was, after all, someone who at one stage of her life had put her sex up for sale. And that for me has always been the ultimate turn-off. I'm not talking so much about simple prostitution, which does have the virtues of a certain honesty. What I have in mind is the corruption of values which can come with wealth and influence. I know, for instance, that in my time I have had to take evasive action against the wives of some rich and powerful football directors.

These were women who had become bored with their husband's involvement in business and football. One director's wife gave me a particularly difficult time, inviting me around to her home for drinks at all sorts of bizarre hours, bumping into me apparently by accident. Eventually, and unsubtly, she managed to get me on my own. The law of averages had insisted that, sooner or later, she must. And she scarcely wrapped anything up. She said that if I made love to her I could forget about my money worries, which at that time were considerable. But if she had had any chance of seducing me they ended with that remark.

I may have some things in my life of which I am not proud, but they do not include the humiliation of being a kept man.

Another director's wife—at another club—pursued me just as hard. But in one sense her approach was different. It was only after the event that she really showed her hand. She emerged as a very dangerous, very nasty lady indeed. She had never been subtle, and at one stage she tended to hang around me. She would turn up at the football ground, fresh from the hairdresser's salon. One night, in a bar, I lost my temper. She had got on my nerves. I told her to get out of the place. Only I didn't put it so politely. I thought that might be the final discouragement. Instead it seemed to have the opposite effect. She applied even more pressure—and I should add that she was not an unattractive woman.

In the end I buckled. I spent an afternoon at her girl friend's cottage. We made love. I wasn't pleased with myself, I sensed that I was letting myself in for some unnecessary trouble. But it was a diverting way to spend the afternoon. She had, at last, caught me in the right

53

mood. I wasn't prepared for her reaction. As I drove away from the cottage she was already dialling out her husband's business number. I suppose it was the time a lot of women ring their husbands to check on what they would like for their evening meal. But she wasn't asking any cosy, domestic questions. She was announcing: "I have just spent the afternoon in bed with Malcolm Allison." Perhaps a psychiatrist might be able to explain her motives, her thinking. It all seemed very sick to me—and I was disgusted with myself for getting involved with such a woman.

A few years later I saw her with her husband and a group of people in a big London hotel. She came up to me, pleasant and talkative. For a moment I couldn't believe it. I didn't know where she had got the nerve to speak to me. I must have put a lot of contempt into my expression. I used an Anglo-Saxon expression which means go away. It was part of my life I wanted to forget. Certainly I had learned an object lesson in the dangers of getting involved with spoilt, bored women.

The impression may be of a Casanova-like series of bedroom romps. But it is a false one. I could never claim to be monkish, but the deceits, the elaborate, sneaky planning involved in a series of affairs has always struck me as absurd. I have walked into restaurants and clubs and seen men I know lurking in dark corners with girls. I have thought: 'How pathetic.'

My early sexual experiences were in Vienna. The first of them was that romantic, almost innocent episode with a butcher's daughter, a story I have already recounted. There was, as a matter of fact, a brief liaison with an Austrian prisoner-of-war's wife. She used to come to a certain dance hall each Saturday afternoon. She was a good-looking girl, very conscious of her appeal. There was a great rivalry among the lads to be the first to take her home. Eventually I danced with her, and she asked: "Would you like to take me home?" When we got to her door she asked me another classic question: "Would you like some coffee?" Instead she opened the bedroom door quite casually and said: "This is where we will sleep." It took me some time to believe this was actually happening to me. I should have been back in camp by midnight, but I thought: "Oh, sod it." At 7.30 I was awakened by an old lady handing me a cup of coffee. It was the girl's grandmother. I was confined to barracks for a week. A small price, I thought.

I suppose my pleasure in female company, my need for its softness, stems to a large extent from the fact that my working life is spent in an entirely male environment. This can be very oppressive. Sometimes you crave simply to talk to someone about anything but football, and this is so much more easily done in the company of women.

I recall an amusing episode in Los Angeles, which flowed entirely from the fact that I felt a desperate boredom in the company of some American FA men. We had dinner at the Roosevelt hotel and were having drinks in a bar-lounge. The place was softly lit and a small group were making music. Across the room—it wasn't very crowded—I saw a very smartly dressed woman sitting alone. I called a waiter and asked him to see if the lady would have a drink with me. He returned to say that she declined with thanks. Feeling slightly desperate with my company, I asked him to see if she would like two drinks. I suppose it wasn't the most subtle overture in the history of courting but it worked. She gave a little smile and I was able to extricate myself from the droning football types. We had a few drinks and danced a little.

She asked me if I would like to go to her apartment for a drink. I said that would be fine and soon we were sweeping through downtown Los Angeles in a yellow Cadillac. Her apartment was superbly furnished, the hi-fi was perfect.

She was a psychiatrist and quite a formidable woman. My approach was quite cautious and eventually I asked if she would drive me back to my hotel. She did so and when we got there I invited her up to my suite for a nightcap. Our conversation had been friendly enough—but I had not

55

exactly forced the pace. As I poured her drink she said to me: "For heaven's sake, where are we going to screw—my place or yours?"

# Chapter Five

## Good Mates

I got married to Beth when I was 26. I broke a vow to myself that I would not take that step until after my 30th birthday. But Beth was the first woman I had cared about. It was a new experience, and though I was hesitant about the responsibilities of marriage and parenthood my feeling for Beth balanced out the fears. I couldn't have married a better girl. Had my illness not made me so restless, I may well have settled into a conventional married life. Certainly I cannot deflect any blame on to Beth. She has always been loyal, forgiving, and also a terrific mother to my four children. She has never nagged me, and, in fact, I cannot recall a single row between us. Not even when I disappeared one Monday afternoon in Manchester. I had gone out to buy some fish for tea. The fishmonger's shop had just closed and I found myself driving into town. I got home at lunch-time the following day. I suppose the fact that my marriage has failed has everything to do with my nature, which is a bit wild, a bit concerned with my own feelings and mood on any one occasion.

When the children were very young I used to worry a lot about the fact that I found it difficult to play the role of the orthodox family man. I used to feel great guilt. That feeling has eased somewhat now. I hope that my children can come to understand that people are built differently, that what is normal behaviour for one man is strange and alien to another.

God knows, these seem bland and simple terms with which to discuss the most difficult problem of a man's life. But behind them I believe there are certain truths. I believe, for instance, that a man will ultimately do what is right for him. He will live in the best way he can. That may be selfish, but it is realistic. Perhaps all I can really say is that I have never lost my respect for a woman who has borne me fine children, and proved an excellent wife.

I was never involved outside my marriage until after the illness that changed so much of my life. The girl was called Suzy. She was blonde. She came into my club off Tin Pan Alley with a girl friend. They had been to the theatre. They were both elegantly dressed and were the sort of girls professional footballers, certainly in those days, did not have too much contact with. Suzy's father owned a factory. She introduced me to some of the subtleties of the high life, talking me through French menus for example. I suppose you could say that Suzy, and her Mayfair world, formed part of my education.

She was the first woman who really tried to dominate me. She knew she had a certain power over me, and at times she applied real pressure. The test of our relationship came when I was offered a contract to coach soccer for a summer in Toronto. She wanted to come along. I said no. It was never the same after that and eventually she married a rather wealthy fellow. But it was a long time before I could forget her: her youth, her sense of personal freedom, lived on with me for a long time. It had been something new in my life and I was reluctant to let it go.

I took the job of managing Plymouth Argyle at the end of that Canadian summer. I found the women of Plymouth very aware of the opposite sex. Perhaps it was because of the town's naval background, but whatever the reason it was sometimes a hard job to keep from being entangled with some woman or another.

One early incident seemed to be typical of the atmosphere in the town. After home games we tended to visit a bar where there was dancing. We would have a few drinks, talk about the game in a nice, relaxing atmosphere.

I began to notice a girl who came into the place regularly. She was attractive enough but the reason I noticed her particularly was that I began to find her staring at me. I'm not talking about the odd, flirtatious glance. She was really giving me a hard look. After one game, which we had won nicely, I was in rather a good mood. I went up to the girl and asked her: "What is it with you, why do you stare at me all the time?" She said simply: "I just want to meet you, talk with you—that's all." I said that I would run her home. I gave her the keys of my car and said that I would be out in a few minutes. In fact I got involved at the bar. The drinks and the conversations were flowing. I got to the car about two hours later. I had forgotten all about the girl. But she was still there, sitting patiently in the front seat of my car. That sort of thing amazed me.

My time in Plymouth, in fact, was a period of evasive tactics. Sometimes, after a few drinks, I might not be so evasive. But there was never any question of getting involved in affairs. I suppose I was still suffering a hangover from Suzy.

At the end of the year I moved to Manchester. In eight years in the city I had two serious affairs, with a model girl called Jeanette ... and Marcia, who owned a gown shop. I probably would not have got involved with Jeanette if she had not been so dismissive when I made my first approach. Repeatedly I asked her out to dinner, and each time she turned me down. Once she said sarcastically: "That's all I need—a fellow like you." That rather turned me on. It was a real challenge.

Eventually I sent her a note along the bar. It simply pleaded with her to come out with me one evening. I drove her home and after quite a bit of stonewalling she took me into her new flat for coffee. She had said: "Coffee is all you are getting." The place was bare. She was waiting for furniture. The following morning I rang up a store in Manchester and ordered, as a matter of urgency, the largest double bed they had. It was sent round to Jeanette's flat that afternoon. It wasn't very subtle ... but it was fun.

We had a good time together. I suppose, to be honest, I really took advantage of Jeanette. She never put me under any pressure. If she saw me out, she saw me. I recall Manchester City making a brief stop in Bangkok airport on the way to a tour in Australia. Jeanette was working at the Bangkok Hilton. She is not one of the top girl employees of Hilton Hotels. I left the aeroplane to try to make a call to her. I kept the plane waiting out on the tarmac but I never looked like breaking through the battery of telephone operators whose only foreign language seemed to be Chinese. When we reached Australia I did call her. It was the end of an affair which had been light-hearted, unforced, the sort which most men hope for and perhaps need at some stage or another.

Jeanette, for whom I used to leave tickets at Manchester City addressed to 'Lady B' was succeeded by a beautiful Brazilian girl called Claudia. I thought of her as the 'Contessa'. She was very dark, very elegant. I met her because the Brazilian ambassador, one warm summer night in London in 1970, had insisted I attended a party at his embassy, I had been appearing on the ITV World Cup Panel and had been quick to salute the brilliance of the winners, Brazil. So had my co-panellists Derek Dougan, Bob McNab and Paddy Crerand.

The ambassador had rung the studio several times so we decided we ought to make an appearance. It was certainly a lavish and lively gathering. I sat down, happy enough to enjoy the music and a couple of drinks. We had been working hard in the studios and it was a pleasant sensation to relax. My attention was drawn to a girl in a white trouser suit, managing, superbly, to cha-cha and play the bongo drums at the same time. It was Claudia. I suggested we should go out for a meal. In the early hours of a Monday morning that is easier said than done. We finished up at the Sportsman's Club in the Tottenham Court Road, eating bacon and eggs.

We saw each other regularly for two years. Sometimes she would slip into Manchester and stay in one of the hotels. Once she came up to Glasgow for a match. Whenever I was in London I used to take her out. As with Jeanette, it was one of those relationships which entirely favoured me. When I was free I expected her to be available.

But she was a proud and haughty girl and it was a situation which could not last indefinitely. It still came as a shock, though, when she told me, over an Italian meal, that she had met another guy and was planning to get married. Absurdly, I was angry. I got up and walked out of the restaurant. My ego had been dented. In the past it had always been I who said when something started and finished.

I suppose the most pleasurable training chore of my career came in 1966 when the beauty queen Jennifer Lowe came to me and said: "Malcolm, I want somebody to get me in good condition for the Miss United Kingdom contest. Would you mind?" It was really like one of those offers from the Mafia. Difficult to refuse.

I had first met Jennifer in rather stormy circumstances at a party given by my friend Noel Cantwell. She came with George Best and Mike Summerbee was in, you might say, a challenging position. Noel and I watched the boys—they were very much boys at the time, and it is a condition I sometimes wonder whether George will ever emerge from—making their moves. She was a very attractive girl and Noel, under the stern gaze of his wife Maggie, asked her to dance. They danced for a while and the gaze of Maggie, and also of George and Mike, got sterner. Jennifer wanted something to eat, so of course Noel took her into the kitchen for some chicken. Maggie walked in behind them and said, quite sweetly, "Would you like a drink, dear?" Jennifer said: "Yes, please," and Maggie emptied a glass all over her.

She's a lovely spirited girl, Maggie. Once when Noel was manager of Coventry I conned a referee into sending off his full back Dietmar Bruck along with Tony Coleman. Coleman had reacted violently to a Bruck foul and I knew he would have to go. So I leaped out of the dug-out, grabbed both players, and said: "That's disgusting, ref, you send them both off and there will be no complaint from me." Maggie said that if she had had a gun in her hand at that moment she would have shot me. And I believe her.

Jennifer used to come down to Maine Road on Thursday afternoon and I used to get her fit in the gym. The groundstaff tended to crowd around a fanlight. I had to tell them about that. It was rather inhibiting. It was a small, pleasant affair.

I was rather more affected by the other beauty queen I got to know very well. Jennifer Gurley, who also won the Miss United Kingdom prize, had a very strong personality along with her striking looks. I nearly fell in love with her. When I went to Italy to consider the Juventus job she was at the back of my mind. Had I said yes to the Italians I may well have taken Jennifer with me—if she would have come. I had no assurance about that. Jennifer Gurley was one of the strongest girls I ever met. There was no question of taking advantage of her. She made it clear that if she submitted to me it would be on her own terms ... and I never met those terms. I do believe, though, that she was fond of me and that if the Italian job had materialised I might have persuaded her to come with me.

At that time I was living on my own in a flat. Pressures had been building on me a bit and I had told my wife Beth that I needed some seclusion. She accepted that. She knew I wasn't living with a girl. Jennifer Gurley did visit me at the flat. She would tidy things up a bit, cook a meal, and we would talk or watch television. It never went further than that. As I said, she was a very strong girl. She offered me great friendship at a rather difficult time in my life and I will always be grateful to her for that.

You will have gathered that I do not put myself up as an authority on women. Often I find their moods and their thoughts elusive, much less predictable than those of most men. I have tended to like them more as I have grown older. No doubt that is because the more experienced you are, the more likely you are to see a woman as an individual rather than some sort of challenge to your masculinity. That sounds very Freudian, but I know it to be my own experience.

I have lived with Serena Williams for nearly two years. We have a flat in Kensington. She says of our relationship: "The thing that makes it work is that we are good mates. That is the important thing."

Serena is very bright, very gay, and she is 20 years younger than me. I met her when she was sixteen, a very striking girl. I had just taken the manager's job at Plymouth. I was staying in a hotel and one evening they were holding a great dinner dance. I believe it was a bookmakers' gathering, which in itself didn't have much appeal for me. I noticed a very striking young girl. Her dress was orange. I remember it reminding me of a Belisha beacon. As she passed me on her way to the cloakroom I took hold of her arm and said: "I would like to take you to dinner, young lady." She said, very coolly, "The name is Williams, third from the bottom of page 262 of the telephone book."

It struck me as a bright, very poised answer. Later she told me that her mind had gone blank and she just couldn't remember her telephone number. I took her out several times and she struck me as an exceptionally intelligent girl with a very strong personality. I offered the opinion that she was wasting her time in Plymouth. She should go to London and get a job there. Later, when I had moved to

63

Manchester, I heard that she had become a Bunny Girl at the Playboy Club. I knew she would do all right. Down the years I used to receive messages from her. In 1972 we began to see each other regularly. She wears a diamond ring that I bought for her one day when the mood took me. It has become inevitable that we will marry.

I know that it is a relationship which might not win widespread approval. But it works for us. We are content in each other's company. And in my experience of life, and the opposite sex, I have learned that that is the most vital thing of all.

# Chapter Six

## The misfit

Looking back down the years I find it easy to recall the days of glory; the high plateaux I walked with Manchester City, a time when I had big and brave footballers playing for me and it seemed that everything I touched turned to gold. There was the exhilarating summer in Canada, when every breeze off Lake Toronto seemed to bring me good news and success. There was also the excitement of starting my managerial career in the gentle town of Bath and then salty Plymouth. And just as vivid are those days of illness when my life seemed to stop.

The difficulty comes when I try to re-trace the indecisive, uncommitted days that lay between those peaks and that valley. They are covered in mist—as they were at the time.

I had worked briefly as a car salesman. I didn't sell many cars. In fact I came to consider it an achievement to report in at the showroom in Warren Street. So I knew, when the gambling days were over, that it was time for something different. Jim Gregory, who was in the motor business in a big way and is now chairman of Queen's Park Rangers, lent me £2,000. It was my stake in the nightclub business. I will never know what strange impulse persuaded me to take the little place on the Charing Cross Road, just off Tin

65

Pan Alley. All my experience had been on the wrong side of the bar.

In fact, the clientele was promising. The place was filled wih show business people, footballers, and villains. The footballers didn't have too much money to spend in those days, but the other groups more than made up for them. If I had had any sort of business instinct, I could have quickly made myself secure for life. Instead I became morose. I spent the profits—and some more besides.

Harry Secombe was perhaps my liveliest customer. His peals of laughter used to echo around the club. Usually he would come in for an afternoon drink and he would bring his chauffeur with him in case he had one too many. Invariably, it was the chauffeur who would get drunk. "Come on boyo, you've had enough," Secombe would announce. And, with a weary expression, he would help him out of the club. When I was able to suppress my frustration at the type of life I was leading, it was possible to have some amusing times. The pop group Temperance Seven, who had a brief but spectacular success, once came in for a few drinks before their evening performance at the Palladium. Temperance Seven! They staggered out to face their public.

Dorothy Squires was a frequent visitor. She was a warm-hearted girl, full of life and with a very strong personality. I liked her gaiety, which came out of her naturally, unlike the forced, alchohol-stimulated variety of some of my other customers. I think she took rather a shine to me. Certainly we got on rather well, and if we didn't have an affair it is true that I went back to her house several times to spend the night. Since those days her life has had a lot of ups and downs, but she is a genuine, gutsy character and I'm sure she has the courage and the optimism to battle through.

Songwriter Michael Carr was another show business type who used to bring some colour into the place. He was a very successful man, with profitable titles like "South of the

Border" and "Red Sails in the Sunset", and he certainly had an appetite for the good life…and getting into domestic strife. Once he came into the club in particular need of a stiff drink. His wife, apparently suspicious of his late arrivals home, had locked him in his bathroom. Wearing only a dressing gown, he had climbed down a drain-pipe and caught a taxi into Tin Pan Alley. He got into his office, paid off the taxi, and sent his secretary out to buy him a complete outfit of clothes. He ordered a double gin and tonic.

I could understand the way creative people like Carr and Secombe relaxed over a drink. It was the other people who amazed me. These were people who had plenty of money but very little idea of how to use it. They would become maudlin and tedious in their drink. They could make "Set them up, barman" the most miserable words in the language.

Certainly the pattern of my own life had never been less satisfactory. I was living the night owl's life. There would be late drinking sessions, bad hangovers, and then the forlorn, early morning trips to Smithfield market to collect steaks for the supper bar.

Nothing crystallised my frustrations more sharply than the day Jimmy Greaves—the great young rising star of Chelsea—spent with me at the club. He was waiting for news of his transfer to Italian football and he had told the agent to ring him at the club. Everything about him told you that this was the most exciting day of his life. He sipped his beer nervously, talking endlessly about what might be in store for him in Milan. He was a bright, optimistic kid untouched by disillusion. He couldn't have guessed how much I envied him his coming journey into a new and exciting world. I had an idea that things might not be as effortless, as magical, as he anticipated, but he would learn such things for himself. When the news came through we broke open champagne. His hopes and his optimism had taken me out of myself.

Ironically, Jimmy Greaves was soon to discover that even a talent as clean and as real as his was no guarantee against the sort of setbacks and frustrations from which I was still suffering. The Italian adventure misfired and quickly Greaves was back in London, playing for Spurs. His career of course was a gem. He was one of the greatest English players of all time, a marvellous goalscorer whose instinct around the penalty area was that of a shark. But he missed what should have been the climax of his professional life—the World Cup Final in 1966. Sir Alf Ramsey preferred the industrious but scarcely comparable Roger Hunt. England won that game and the decision became a footnote in the history of the game. Four years later, when he was in the twilight of his career, I tried to sign him for Manchester City. But instead he became small change in the deal which took Martin Peters from West Ham to Tottenham Hotspur. I had planned a more spectacular and fitting climax than that.

At about the same time that Jimmy Greaves was moving into his luxury apartment in Milan I was driving down to Romford, Essex, on a strange football mission. I was seeking to become the first professional player to sign a contract which undertook to pay no money. Jack Chisholm, the Southern League club's manager, shifted uneasily in his little office when I told him I wanted to play for his club. He pleaded an empty kitty, claiming that he probably had the smallest wage bill in all of football.

I told Chisholm: "Jack I'm spending my days and nights in a smoky night club in London. It's not my scene, I want to get the feel of football again... I think I might be able to do a job for you out on the pitch. I don't want any money. I want to make a start in breaking away from this nightclub business." So I became the first amateur professional to commute out of the West End. I played seven reserve games for Romford before Chisholm sent his right hand man down to watch me. He reported that I was the best player in the team and I was immediately promoted to the first team. I kept my place throughout the season. And I got back my appetite for football.

I think I saved myself with that season at Romford. It put into perspective the flashy, big-time-Charlie days on the racecourse and in the nightclub. I had got some sort of basic satisfaction back into my life. I was also reassured by my ability to last a vigorous 90-minute match. Illness had eaten into my confidence more than I had realised. It was revived in the company of great football characters like Trevor Ford and Ted Ditchburn.

Jack Chisholm was a warm, engaging type and we had a lot of laughs. Once we achieved a major transfer coup. We were playing at Worcester City. Before the game we learned that two Everton Directors were down to sign the Worcester ouside left. The financial health of Romford was always hazardous and we wondered about our chances of pushing our own man, Peter Cavanagh, into the shop window. We agreed it was remote. The lad was useful enough, but certainly not the sort you would back to walk into a First Division side. But very early in the game I realised we did have a chance. The man marking our winger was hopeless. He was a tall, skinny guy and not very bright. I was playing left half and I spent most of the afternoon pinging the ball over the full back's head. It was easy for our winger. He was quick and he could cross the ball accurately and with the service I supplied he completely outclassed the Worcester winger. He hit the bar twice and scored a goal. Everton signed him for £1,500, played him in a few games, then allowed him to disappear.

Just as happily, I recall being booed and jeered at Walthamstow Avenue. We were awarded a penalty in the last minute. I had become nicely unpopular with the crowd and when I was told to take the kick I went up to the keeper and pointed to the corner of the net I intended to hit. Against a chorus of boos, I found my target. But the referee ordered the kick to be retaken and this time I indicated to the crowd where I meant to put the ball. They really hissed and howled as I struck the ball home. It was no more than mild horseplay, but I think it showed that I was beginning to enjoy myself again.

Cambridge University completed my recovery. I was invited to coach the soccer team. I did go there with certain misgivings. I was conscious of my working class background and uncertain about the sort of reception I would receive. Certainly the dressing rooms of English football were not the ideal preparation for such an apparently cloistered world. But those apprehensions were dispelled as I drove into the city on a sunny, summer morning.

The place was alive with cycling undergraduates. Two of them clad in gowns and with text books balancing on their handlebars, collided and sprawled right in front of my bonnet. I jammed on my brakes and sat back, waiting for the punch-ups and curses which might have followed such a collision in the Old Kent Road.

They dusted themselves down very quietly. One turned to the other, saying: "I'm terribly sorry, old chap." The other replied: "Not at all, old chap, entirely my fault. Very sorry." Then they both turned slowly and said to me, almost in one voice, "Terribly sorry." That was pure revelation. Later, when I arrived at the athletic grounds, the captain of Soccer came up to me, shook hands, and said: "We're all very thrilled that you're coming to work with us. We've heard a lot about you and we're ready to start when you are."

I doubt that anything has given me more immediate pleasure and satisfaction than the willingness of those boys to listen, and then work right to the edge of their ability. After our training sessions they would take me to a coffee house or perhaps a pub and we would talk for hours about the game. They were bright, very intelligent young people and they brought with them some very beautiful girls.

Occasionally I would be invited to a cocktail party at one of the colleges. I recall admiring a very imposing portrait of a former Bursar of the college, and being told: "Oh yes, he was a great character. He did have one flaw in a very distinguished career. Over the years he nicked about £18,000 worth of college funds. But we cannot take his picture off the wall. We wouldn't want to make a fuss about something like that." It seemed that the quality of forgiveness shown by those crashed cyclists was an ingrained thing at Cambridge.

We had a successful team. Whatever training routines I laid down were followed slavishly. I would travel back to London knowing that my instructions would be followed. And we won the big one, the Varsity match at Wembley.

Later that day, over celebration drinks at the Varsity Club in Piccadilly, I was invited to take over Pegasus, the combined Cambridge and Oxford team. The offer was made by Tommy Thompson, the scientist-football fanatic who was knighted and was to emerge as such a powerful figure along the corridors of the FA at the time of Sir Alf Ramsey's sacking in 1974. But the offer, which on the face of it was a great honour, had unacceptable strings. Thompson boomed at me "You will train the players, Allison, and I will pick the team." I do not warm to people who address me by my surname, and I was even less disposed towards being ordered around by a man who, for all his intellect, was very much the football amateur. I told Thompson, in effect, to stuff Pegasus. I regretted the break with the University boys and I knew that I would miss those days filled with enthusiasm and companionship at Cambridge.

But I sensed the first stirrings of my career as a professional coach and manager. Certainly I knew I had to get back into the professional game. Inevitably, the night club was beginning to founder. I had neglected the business, but it was neglect born of boredom and something approaching distaste.

The nightclub had imposed an unnatural existence on me. I had been going to bed at the wrong time, waking at the

71

wrong time, and my reactions and senses had been dulled. Playing football at Romford and coaching at Cambridge had been in such contrast, filling me with such pleasure and satisfaction that I knew I would be wide open to the first serious offer I received from a football club.

Bob Pennington, a football writer on the Daily Express, had written a timely piece. He asked how it was that one of the three best coaches in the country was out of League football. Pennington's piece did not trigger a landslide of clubs at my door. But he did get the ball rolling. Bert Tann, the manager of Bristol Rovers, rang with a coaching offer... and Southern League Bath City wanted me as their manager.

I had always vowed that I would never get involved in non-league football. It had always seemed a bit of a wasteland to me, a place for youngsters who would probably never be good enough and broken, cynical old pros. But Romford had softened my attitude and I decided to drive to Bath and take a look around.

Unfortunately I had a vague idea that Bath was no more than two hours west of Shepherd's Bush. The result was that I was two hours late for my interview with the President, local businessman Arthur Mortimore. But he gave me the job... and confided that his big ambition in life was to see a First Division team play on the Bath ground. In these days when non-league clubs like Leatherhead and Wimbledon have proved that mystique and myth can be shattered by forceful, courageous football on First Division grounds, Mortimore's ambition may now seem a little inflated. But it was obviously a very real and vital thing to him and I said that I would see what I could do.

I spent my first day at the club visiting the players at factories and farms. I met the captain Tony Book on a building site. He told me he was a stonemason and when I asked: "What's that, a high class bricklayer?" his tanned, strong face broke into a smile. I knew we would get on, though I could not have guessed quite how well. There were some other good pros there, people like Ian McFarlane, now assistant manager of Manchester City under Book, and Charlie "Cannonball" Fleming. But the team were struggling, bottom of the League with three matches to play.

All the players were on £13 a week. My first move was to arrange a productivity deal. I got their money up to £15 and they agreed to come in for extra training. Because of their different working hours I found myself dealing with small groups of players and I immediately saw the advantage of this. It enabled me to develop my ideas on specialised coaching.

I also wanted a bit more skill in the side. I signed the former Portsmouth star Len Phillips on a free transfer from Chelmsford. He was already 41 and some people at Bath thought I was mad. But I have never been inclined to place men in any sort of category, especially in the matter of age. In my football career I have seen 30-year-olds trembling before they went out to play a game, and in the same dressing room a 17-year-old might be quietly chewing gum, very sure of himself and what he has to do. I also know of men in the fifties who are in superb physical shape, and others who are shot through before they reach the age of 30. Phillips was in lovely shape and he relished this late reprieve to his professional career. He gave us a lot of class, a lot of touch, and indirectly he may have influenced me in my cultivation of Tony Book's career.

When I moved to Plymouth the following summer I took Book with me. I paid the club £1,500. After I gave the cheque to one of the Bath directors, a former player, Geoff Fox, he smiled and said: "Don't you realise he is nearly 31?" I didn't know what that was supposed to mean. But I do recall that Fox's half-sneering expression flickered back into my mind five years later when Tony Book received the Football Writers' award as 'Player of the Year'. He shared the title with Dave Mackay, a player who had had his best days when Book first entered the world of full-time professional football.

I take no credit for sponsoring Book's late run for glory. I was simply astonished by his quality the first time I saw him play. He was one of the best and quickest defenders I had seen in any class of football. There was a timing, poise, and a tremendous recovery rate. I knew too that he looked after himself. I reckoned there was 10 years of professional playing life in him. It was a natural thing for me to take him on to Manchester City when I left Plymouth.

I have so many rich memories of Tony Book urging Manchester City to the great triumphs. He even scored a crucial goal against Everton late in the season 1967/68, a goal which helped push us into that spectacular run on the rails for our championship win. He was tremendous in two successful Wembley appearances and also in the Prater Stadium, Vienna, when we won the European Cup-Winners Cup. Book's playing career in fact served as an example to many professionals. Because he got into the game so late, he never lost his appreciation of the rewards it was bringing him. His dedication was total.

There is just one touch of irony about our relationship. It occurred quite recently when I was desperately seeking to strengthen the Crystal Palace forward line. A few years ago I signed for Manchester City a boy called Barney Daniels. He cost £1,000 from the local non-league side Mossley. I had heard that he was doing well in the reserves and when Book dropped Mike Summerbee for one home game, Daniels came in and scored two goals. But quickly he lost his place in the City first team. I rang Tony one morning, saying that I was in a tight situation and could I have Barney Daniels on loan for a month. He said he would ring me back. He did, and told me that he couldn't loan Daniels, but I could have him for £40,000.

I didn't have £40. It was one of those amusing things which happen so often in football. On the surface there is much sentiment. Beneath that surface the reality is harder.

It was a somewhat different world at Bath. The team

74

began to develop confidence and I was able to deliver to Arthur Mortimore his dream of squaring up against a First Division club. We drew Bolton Wanderers in the FA Cup and I don't think I have ever seen such pleasure on a man's face as when Arthur Mortimore heard that draw. He said to me: "That's it, I don't care what happens now. We have brought a First Division team to Bath." In fact we went very close to knocking out Wanderers. Against men of the calibre of Francis Lee, Wyn Davies, and Freddie Hill we played aggressively and I think they were very grateful to settle for a 1-1 draw. Bolton had come down with a little bit of bombast. Their manager Bill Ridding had sneered at the fact that our part-time secretary had sent Bolton their Cup tickets in a biscuit tin. I was offended by that trivial point. Bath was a little club without pretension. And it was filled with people who lived for football, who loved it for its own sake rather than any great personal prestige they could draw from it.

We lost the replay at Bolton by 3-0. But we played well, we presented them with a few problems and on the journey back to the West Country there was only laughter and the satisfaction that comes when you have gone into good company and earned their respect.

I left Bath as reluctantly as I did Cambridge. I think I sensed that it would be a long time before I worked for a man as straightforward and as appreciative as Arthur Mortimore. His hand had always gone straight to his pocket when the club needed new gear, or when the bank had made a threatening noise. He was absolutely committed to the game and his own small club. And it was an expensive commitment, one I was soon to compare very favourably with those of many of the directors I met and worked with in the Football League.

Of course there are exceptions. One reason, the most important in fact, which persuaded me to turn down the offer of Manchester City to return in season 73/74 was the attitude of Crystal Palace chairman Ray Bloys. Through all the problems he had shown great faith and loyalty to me. And when the crunch came I felt I could not walk out on him. What does disgust me is the approach of the many directors who are in the game for the fringe benefits of local prestige, free travel and entertainment, and perhaps even business contacts. They have a superficial understanding of the game, and their judgments can be appallingly wide of the mark. It can be a sickening spectacle to see some of these characters riding waves of success, or howling for the blood of a manager, without any sort of grasp on the basis of success or failure.

It is also true that throughout my career in football I have been conscious of the inter-play of jealousy at boardroom level. It is astonishing to consider the level of pettiness that successful businessman, who have shoved and pushed their way into positions of wealth and influence, can descend to once they get their feet into the door of a football club. Often you feel the place has become a playground for their second childhood.

At Bath, where the game was always the most important thing, I didn't feel this at all. And because of this it was the perfect place to gather up again the pieces of my career as a professional football man. I may not have been in the main stream again, but the tide was beginning to flow.

# Chapter Seven

## The go-getter

In the spring of 1964 it seemed that once again the world was at my feet. As I walked down the Strand on Cup Final morning I felt strong, relaxed—and in demand. I had, for a start, the sort of good, tight schedule which always gives me a sense of well-being.

First, I had to go to the Savoy to meet the directors of Plymouth Argyle. Apparently they had followed my work at Bath and were on the point of asking me to take over as their manager. If this was so, it was a major step forward. Then I would go up to Wembley to watch my old club West Ham meet Preston North End. Finally, I would drive to Heathrow for a night plane to Canada, where I was to spend the summer organising the football ambitions of a Greek millionaire called Steve Stavros in Toronto.

The meeting at the Savoy went well. I found the Plymouth directors with their chairman Ron Blindell sipping drinks in a lush suite. Even when Blindell told me that they had other candidates to interview I felt confident that I would get the job. I explained briefly my experience, my coaching qualifications, and all that I thought was needed if English club football was to make any sort of progress. They listened attentively and said they would let

77

me know. Apparently they decided to give me the job as soon as I left the room and one of the directors was sent after me to bring me back. But he missed me and I flew off to Canada not knowing in which part of the West Country I would be operating the following winter.

But that was a detail which I knew would resolve itself. Sometimes in life you can sense that you are on a winning streak, and this was such a time. The challenge in Toronto was beautifully simple. Stavros, who enjoyed football but was more interested in making money, wanted to exploit the ethnic rivalries in the lakeside city. There were large elements of Germans, Poles, and Italians and they were all represented by strong teams in the city league. Stavros wanted me to develop his side, Toronto City, so that it would draw good support from the big English and Scottish communities.

The question of how you whip up support, and then titillate and excite it, had always fascinated me. It is an aspect of sports presentation at which the North Americans have always excelled. Some of it is frankly corny. But I like the recognition that it is not enough to present two teams playing 90 minutes of football. Supporters have to be drawn into the drama of the thing in a more positive way than merely being invited to buy a team scarf or a rosette.

Certainly Stavros made it clear that he wanted very close identification between the team and their supporters. I saw a lot of potential in our league match with the Italian club team named patriotically enough, Italia. The custom in Toronto was the continental one of the teams waving to all sections of the crowd before the start. I told my team to wave to every section except the Italians, adding: "Delay that until the moment you score your first goal."

It was a simple, you might say crude, ploy but it worked wonderfully well. The game became an event, a crusade; from behind the wire barriers the Italian fans whistled and chanted endlessly. And they had Anglo-Saxon opposition from across the pitch. We opened the score neatly and my players ran across to the Italians waving and blowing kisses. The Italians had been incensed enough by the earlier snub. Now they raged and howled for our blood.

But we never relaxed our grip on the game, finishing 3-1 winners. After the match some of my players came to me asking where I thought it would be suitable to celebrate. I suggested the most famous Italian restaurant in Toronto, a place called George's. Enthusiasm for the celebration faded and in the end I went to George's with just Nigel Sims and another player, Norman Sykes.

Inside the restaurant there was the usual crescendo of noise to be heard whenever Italians gather to eat, drink, play music, sing, and discuss football and women. But as soon as we walked into the place there was absolute silence. The little group stood poised between notes and there were many suspended strands of spaghetti.

Quite suddenly all the diners got up from their seats and started to clap and shout: "Bravo, English." A posse of waiters led us to a table, bottles of fine Chianti were uncorked, and we ate magnificently. The manager refused to take our money. It was a superb evening, filled with laughter and lots of football talk. I think it may have been something to do with the fact that I had at least brought a little bit of colour into the local football scene. Certainly I had tried to make it clear that I was only interested in trying to get the game over to the Canadian public.

I was lucky in that I had some good, experienced players in the side, including Book, Johnny Brooks, Nigel Sims and Ted Purdom. We didn't lose a game that summer, winning the title with 15 points from eight games and also the Challenge Cup.

It was a marvellously exhilarating summer. And I recall that there was plenty of money. Stavros was not ungenerous if he got the right results and with the help of some nice wins at the Toronto race track I was able to live extravagantly. I stayed in a swish apartment block overlooking the lake and as I write this it occurs to me that I left without paying my final bill. I don't feel too badly about it. It only amounted to about 200 dollars and I'm sure Stavros would have picked up that tab. He probably got it back on the empties.

I was once carrying enough cash to outbid Richard Burton and Liz Taylor for waiter attention at Toronto's most luxurious night spot, the Swiss Bear. I had been irritated by the service, which was inevitably sluggish when you considered the number of people hovering around the Burtons' table. I snapped to a waiter: "Give me half a dozen bottles of champagne, send some to the band, and here's a handful of dollars for the head waiter." Service improved. Someone in my party wanted the girl singer to do 'Hello Dolly'. She said it was not on her list. So I bought some more champagne and she ended up singing 'Hello Dolly' six times.

I know that it all sounds rather flash. Some of my close friends describe my behaviour with money as stupid. But it is something more than an urge to be the big man. I suppose deep down I have such a liking for happy occasions. And certainly in Toronto that summer I felt again that I had something to celebrate. I had come into Toronto and done a good job. I had fresh evidence that I could get players to respond to me. The undergraduate footballers of Cambridge were one thing. But now I had done it with hardened pros both in Bath and in Canada.

It was a good feeling. Every man needs to feel that he has a certain strength, an ability which sets him apart. It was such knowledge which coloured my days in Canada. Those days of brisk, rewarding work on the lakeside and the nights of relaxation merge into one warm afterglow.

Plymouth sent me a telegram requesting another interview, but suggesting strongly that I had got the job. I went straight to the airport. Customs men at Heathrow were staggered when I insisted that I had travelled from Canada without luggage. I was impatient to involve myself in the next challenge. I quickly agreed terms with

Plymouth, and then immediately turned about and flew to Toronto for the run-in to the title.

All I knew about Plymouth was that there was much work to do there. They had avoided relegation to the Third Division the previous season by one-hundredth of a goal. But that was a situation which I liked. The really killing pressure comes when you inherit a team which has been really successful, as Wilf McGuiness and Frank O'Farrell did at Manchester United, and Brian Clough at Leeds. It is also a psychological fact that a new manager can expect at least a profitable first month, when players are eager to impress him and the sheer uncertainty of the new situation creates a sort of productive tension. I knew that I could immediately strengthen the team by bringing in my man Tony Book and playing him in the Italian 'sweeper' style. That would tidy up the defence, give a base of security. It would be a sound, if unspectacular start.

In fact, I could scarcely have made a less impressive start at Plymouth's Home Park ground. I felt in good form as I drove my ramshackle Borgward into the car park. I was bronzed from the Canadian summer, the sky was blue, and the birds were singing. But the reception was cold. Two detectives were waiting to see me in my office. They had come to arrest me on the matter of £94 worth of unpaid parking tickets.

As I spoke to them I could see, through a glass partition, the horrified expressions on the faces of the club secretary and two girl typists. What a way to start a push for fame. I wrote out a cheque and wondered vaguely what happens to you if you pass the law a rubber one. Miraculously, or mercifully, I'm not sure which, the bank passed the cheque—and I stayed out of prison.

But at that moment I think it dawned on Plymouth Football Club that their new manager was a bit of a lad. I think some of the board were a little perturbed that they might have introduced some sort of a tearaway to the town. Certainly there were no early invitations to join the Rotary

Club. Some were scandalised that I wasn't always at home by 10 o'clock. And inevitably I got involved in the boardroom intrigues. One director, Doug Fletcher, never forgave me for siding with the chairman Daniels on one issue. The Board announced to the press that I had £100,000 to spend. In fact it was £50,000. There were some lively board meetings—and it seemed that the only thing they hadn't got against me was the way I ran their team.

One aspect of Plymouth I wanted to exploit was the sea and the glorious countryside. I wanted a team of super-fit footballers. My first question after emerging from the grip of Plymouth C.I.D. was: "Where is the best beach around here?" I ordered up the team coach and we drove to the beach. It was 15 miles away, down winding narrow lanes. I took a formidable amount of stick that first morning. There were comments like: "Did you remember your bucket and spade, Fred?" Eventually we settled for the Whitesands beach. To get down on to it we had to scramble across 200 feet of cliff. I loaded them with weights, equipment, packed lunches. After morning training, we would have lunch on the beach, a swim, and then more training. It was tough work—but also a superb preparation for the coming season.

Very quickly it was clear that survival was no longer Plymouth Argyle's problem. The question was whether we could win something. For most of the season we were in a challenging position for promotion to Division One. And first division Leicester City had to battle to beat us in the semi-final of the League Cup. As I anticipated, Book brought immense strength into the side. His leadership alone was of immense value. And his reading of the game, his speed and sharpness, spread security through the side. Nicky Jennings and Norman Piper were emerging as very talented young players, and goals were coming from Frank Lord—later my coach at Crystal Palace—and Mike Trebilcock, who two years afterwards became Everton's FA Cup hero against Sheffield Wednesday.

I evolved a system of play which was based on people striking from strong midfield situations. We knocked Stoke City, Sheffield United and Northampton out of the League Cup before falling to Leicester City in the semi-final. Tony Waddington complained that we had played very negatively. What he hadn't been able to fathom properly was that I was the first English manager to play a definite sweeper. I was lucky that most English teams had not then given any thought to the problem of beating the 'extra defender' ... and also that in Book I had the perfect exponent of the job. We played Bury twice over the Easter holiday, and they were no wiser about what we were doing the second time we played them.

What killed us was an injury to Frank Lord. It took away a lot of our momentum, and that momentum had been considerable. We were second in the table at Christmas and looking very threatening. Everything I tried seemed to come off. I played a 16-year-old called Richard Reynolds in the FA Cup against Derby County and he scored two goals. But the Lord injury broke the run. I made my first big tactical mistake in football. Instead of pushing a reserve into Lord's place and asking the other players to retain as much of their rhythm as they could in the new circumstances, I tried to re-organise the side. What happened was that I was weakening more than one position. We began to lose ground, finishing eighth in the League. There was also the fact that deep down I realised the players were not quite good enough to get up to the First Division.

Football director and manager relationships follow a classic pattern. When there is success the differences of personality and attitude are submerged, but they rise quickly enough to the surface once the ball starts to roll against you. Plymouth sacked me at the end of that first season. I wasn't shocked—or really surprised. I had given my support to the chairman, and he was involved in constant, bickering battles with his boardroom colleagues. I became an issue. Some felt my style was too aggressive, too flamboyant for Plymouth. My arrogance offended some of them and I had started to get into trouble with the FA over my onslaughts against referees. There was also the fact that I didn't exactly lead a monkish life. The Plymouth directors wanted their club to be a success, but they were not prepared to pay the price of having a character like Malcom Allison around.

Ironically, they came to me four years later—when my Manchester City team had become the most attractive in England—and asked me to go back to Plymouth. They offered to double my City salary. They said they felt I was the only man who could get Plymouth moving again. There was no way that they could have persuaded me to return to the West Country. A few months later the Italian giants Juventus were to make their offer seem like the smallest of change. I declined Plymouth politely—but I must admit that the fact that they came back gave me a lot of satisfaction.

It was as though the one question mark aginst my short but spectacular career as coach and manager had been removed. I had re-organised Cambridge University soccer and won the Varsity match twice. I had lifted up Bath City, won a championship and cup for Toronto, and now Manchester City were poised to add the FA Cup to the championship they had carried off the previous season. Plymouth, where I knew I had done well in every football sense, had nagged at me. But here were the burghers of Plymouth pleading with me to allow them to get out the fatted calf and welcome back the prodigal.

In fact, I was a good deal less than shattered by the Plymouth sacking. That instinct I had had the previous spring, when I swept through the Savoy en route for Canada, held good. Within days of my dismissal I had been offered three jobs. The Amsterdam club Blue-White wanted me to take over their team and they were offering good money. Raich Carter, then manager of Middlesbrough, wanted me to be his coach. And while I was making arrangements to travel to Middlesbrough, I rang Joe Mercer to congratulate him on his return to football. He had just celebrated his emergence from a lot of nervous illness by accepting the challenge of rebuilding Manchester City. He suggested that on my way to Middlesbrough I might call in at Maine Road.

All my life I had lived in awe of the great players. I knew enough about football and myself to understand that however hard I might try that role would never have been assigned for me. Now it was a flattering thing to be recognised and valued by men of the calibre of Carter and Mercer. Mercer had seen me work at the Lilleshall centre and my Plymouth team had embarrassed Middlesbrough on their own ground. Both obviously felt that I could help them reshape their new, once-powerful clubs.

I sensed that I would never complete my journey to Middlesbrough. I was ready to make the big push with Manchester City.

# Chapter Eight

## The Italian job

In the cold, dreary weeks which started 1975, with the rain slanting in over the rows of rooftops around Selhurst Park, my club Crystal Palace faltered badly in the effort to win promotion from Division Three. We lost successive matches at my old ground Charlton and at Aldershot, and these were sickening blows. It was a sharp crisis and it called into question all the work I had been doing since I left Manchester City in the spring of 1973. It made me feel a certain amount of nostalgia for the old days and, particularly, for the summer of 1969. I did ask myself: "Will I ever be so strong again?"

I'm talking about that summer when the Italians rolled out a magic carpet and invited me to fly to the stars.

Their emissary was the best-dressed journalist I have ever seen. He wore a superb silk shirt and his cuffs were kept in place by gold bracelets. His suit was immaculately cut, and his very presence suggested a lot of money. He was covering AC Milan's European Cup semi-final game with Manchester United and he had told the reception girl at Manchester City that he had to have 'very important' talks with Mr. Allison. As soon as he walked into my office I sensed he wasn't looking for a team sheet. He told me that he was 'empowered' to invite me to think about joining Juventus as their manager. Money was no object—either for myself or for the building of a new team. I could virtually write my own contract—and budget. Juventus were determined to be top team in Europe. They had scoured Europe for a man to lead them to power. And, after much thought, they had decided on me.

On that grey, wet afternoon in Manchester he was painting a dazzling picture. As the journalist, speaking very precise English, went on to explain the recent history of the club, its potential and its plans, I knew that very soon I would be facing the biggest decision of my career. I knew that what he was offering repreented, at the very least, financial security. Manchester City had not been the most generous club with their money and once again I had debts. My car, for instance, had been recently reclaimed by a finance company. But money has always been a marginal thing with me. More importantly, could I do a job in Italy? Was the gamble too great? And why should I leave Maine Road after doing so much to build one of the best sides in Europe? But against these hard questions was the knowledge that the Italians did know how to reward success. They had style and they had tremendous resources.

I thanked the journalist for calling and said that of course I was interested. I told him I would wait for further contact. It came on a heath in one of the more deserted parts of Lancashire, near Preston. The new contact man was Gigi Peronace, who had persuaded Denis Law and John Charles to try their luck in Italy. He was very anxious that news did not break, and he set up the meeting with a secrecy that suggested he was beginning to believe the publicity about him being the world's number one 'Soccer Spy'. He told me that the business was moving forward. Peronace wanted me to fly to Turin. At that time I was deeply involved in Manchester City's build-up to the Cup final with Leicester City. I didn't want this business to cut across these preparations, so we agreed that I would fly out to Italy after the final.

Italy cast a long shadow over that approach to Wembley. I was confident that we would beat Leicester. Tony Coleman, my tearaway winger, had got involved in a fight on the weekend before the final and this injury had to be nursed and concealed. But beyond that there were no alarms. We stayed in Weybridge and it was a confident camp. I knew that in Mike Summerbee, Francis Lee, and Colin Bell I was carrying too much ammunition for the Leicester manager Frank O'Farrell. In fact, Leicester, who were committed to the Second Division the following season, played with a lot of bite and much flair. Allan Clarke played particularly well and his running, plus the threat of the veteran Andy Lochead, put us under some unexpected pressure. But Summerbee, who was quietly murdering young David Nish along the right flank, put in a superb burst to the line and his centre was hammered in by Neil Young. It was a good final, closer than I expected, and I should have enjoyed that triumph like no other. But I couldn't get the challenge, the bait of Juventus out of my mind.

At the victory banquet at the Café Royal I looked at the faces of my players; Lee, slightly drunk but full of humour and devil, Summerbee, puckish and dry, and the quiet, almost sombre Bell. And I wondered how a football man in his right mind could consider leaving players of this quality.

There had been some problems with all three players. Once I put it around, in a way that I knew would get back, that I considered Summerbee a spent force. I said that he had changed from being a country boy into a city slicker in two weeks, and that his football had gone. He brought his widowed mother, who had been married to a very tough professional footballer, to my house to tell me tat the Summerbees were fighters—and that he would prove me wrong. Of course he did. Or thought he did. When Francis Lee went through a phase of believing that he was the ultimate footballer, shortly after he had been picked by

England, I suggested to certain football writers that I was on the point of dropping him. I left him in suspense all one Saturday morning in Newcastle. He had a terrific game. Bell needed encouragement to believe in himself in those days. He didn't realise quite how good he was. So I christened him Nijinksy and said that he was the best European player since Puskas. And he can still prove me right on that. But the point was that we were through the difficult phase. We knew each other's strengths and weaknesses. We could make things work.

Was it possible to surrender all this apparent certainty in exchange for a wide open future, even though a blank cheque was part of the deal? There are certain things that money cannot buy. You cannot buy the sort of slogging work which these players had subjected themselves to for years, or the slowly dawning knowledge of a player's strengths and weaknesses. The more I thought about it the more insoluble it became. And increasing the pressure was the awareness that this was probably the one big chance I would get to exploit personally the run of success which we had been having. However strong and secure you may feel in football, there is alway the risk of some sort of ambush. If I was to cash in my chips, this, certainly, was the time to do it.

I was no nearer to reaching a decision when my plane touched down in Turin. Reporters and cameramen lined the apron. When the doors of the plane were swung open the press charged in a solid pack. I felt good. I was dressed in a light blue suit and I had on white shoes. Before leaving London I recalled the appearance of the first contact man, the journalist, and I didn't want to feel under-dressed. That sort of thing can make you feel at a disadvantage. I think I made a good first impression. At least I can immodestly report the comment of the Juventus president. Apparently he turned to a Daily Express cameraman, Jimmy Milne, and said: "What a man!" Milne reported this to me and it didn't do my confidence any harm. I felt that the next week or so would be one of the most crucial periods of my life and I wanted to be on top of myself, making the right reactions and, ultimately, the right decision.

The Juventus officials put me in a red Ferrari and we swept in a great cavalcade, to the club offices in the city centre. That drive might have been part of a James Bond spectacular. Cameramen were getting shots from the back of motorbikes and newsreel men were racing alongside, platforms swaying. It was, even for my taste for the spectacular, all a bit overwhelming. They told me Juventus were playing against a Third Division side 15 miles away. Would I like to go along? The cavalcade re-formed and we roared to the match. We had a sort of heaving, chaotic press conference at half-time. What players would I buy? What players would I sack? How much money was I demanding? The pressure on me was rising, minute by minute.

I was being given an incredibly hard sell in a not too subtle way. When they took me into a fourth boardroom, as full of silverware as the other three, I wanted to burst out laughing. It all seemed to much. The medical centre was superb. It might have been transplanted from the Mayo clinic. But no one had got round to talking about money. It seemed as though they wanted to give me time to soak up fully the splendour of Juventus football club.

On the following morning I went down to see the players training. A crowd of 5,000 turned up to take a look at me. Everywhere I went there was this strange, incredible intensity. Later in the week I went to a friendly match at the great stadium, and saw Juventus lose 2-1. The officials were bitter about losing the game, and the fans hissed and jeered. It was all on a different level to anything I had experienced before. The Juventus team was valued at nearly £2 million. And some officials were saying that if I took the job I should sack the lot and start again. There were already moves afoot to pay £400,000 for the Naples goalkeeper Dino Zoff. There seemed a deep urge to spend money, to be seen to be doing things to improve the team, and I imagined that this would be the most difficult phase of the job. In my career I had always been reluctant to be pressured into doing things I wasn't sure about, and here there would be a hurricane of pressure at the first set-back.

On the third day we started to talk terms. I was to be offered a two-year contract at £20,000 a year tax free. Added to this would be a guaranteed bonus of £10,000 a year. I was intrigued about the payment of 'guaranteed' bonuses, but they said it was a Juventus 'custom'. They also pointed out that the President had a habit of calling around on a Monday morning following a good victory. And he liked to express his satisfaction with a little cheque of £1,000. In the past I had talked with Helenio Herrerra, the 'black magician' of Italian football, and he had told me that the really important thing in Italy was to make sure of your contract. There were clearly no problems in this respect. Agnelli said: "If you are disturbed about being lonely here, you can have a private aeroplane. Why not fly your friends over each week-end?" I did suggest that I might have John Charles, a great hero among the Italian public, working for me but they seemed cool about this. What was clear was that they wanted me badly and that I had only to sign a piece of paper to solve all my financial problems for the foreseeable future.

I was beginning to waver. Deep down I had felt the odds were against my leaving Maine Road. The Italians had flattered me and I was genuinely fascinated by the way they did things. There was a great sweep and grandeur about it. Their football might be appallingly negative and their methods very cynical, but their passion and their commitment elevated the game into the realms of an incredibly colourful fantasy.

They began to press me for a decision. I don't generally take much time to reach a decision. I am a man of impulse and instinct, but this was something different. Nothing, before or since, has taken so much of my time and thought.

I pleaded for a few days. I had with me my own English

'press corps', including my friend, Paul Doherty, the Manchester-based free-lance journalist, Alan Thompson of the Daily Express and his cameraman partner Jimmy Milne. The boys thought it would be a good idea to drive the short distance to the French Riviera where I could 'make up my mind'. And Paul Doherty wanted to see Rome. We had a good day in Menton and a lively trip to Rome. And I got involved briefly with an exotic strip-tease dancer at a Turin nightclub. She was a Hungarian of very theatrical instincts. I remember walking down the main street of Turin with her in the small hours as she took her chihuahua for a walk. She had a bow around its neck and when I took her for dinner the following evening the dog came along. And had Chateaubriand! I drank milk in the nightclub. Milk laced with brandy.

The diversions scarcely deflected me from the central problem of what to do. My thoughts poured over all the possibilities. And in retrospect I know that I was right in one of my conclusions. I sensed that this was a now-or-never situation. The odds against my being offered such a job in the future were very high.

One point bothered me above all. I hated the way they played and I knew I would have to try to change the system. And the risks involved in that operation would be enormous. I just didn't have the time to scrap everything and start afresh. The Agnellis, and their equally impatient fans, would not stand for that. And after years of defence-dominated football they might also be at a loss to understand what I was trying to achieve. The more I looked at Italian football the more incomprehensible it became. They had so many marvellous players, Rivera, Mazzola, and Riva, and yet their impact on world football had been feeble since their great days in the thirties. All the resources, all the fanaticism, apparently, couldn't create a genuine thrust.

I was perturbed, too, about my ability to communicate with the players. I don't mean basic football language. That would have been no problem. I have worked classes at Lilleshall involving 13 different nationalities. But in Turin I would be attempting to do more than merely change a system of play. I would be trying to get inside their skins and their brains. I really had to talk to them—and this seemed a real problem.

I reached the point where I felt that my best strategy would probably be to work gradually. The idea would be to influence the younger players in a new style of play and thought so that when we had practice games, and fresh blood came into the first team, a new force would become apparent. It was a general, half-formed idea, and I was conscious that it probably needed more time than I had at my disposal.

It was over dinner in Rome that I decided it wasn't on. Absurdly, it suddenly occurred to me that I didn't like Turin. I tried to imagine myself enjoying my work and life in the place and I couldn't. Had I got involved with Juventus and achieved some rhythm of work that feeling, almost certainly, would have disappeared. I had come to love Manchester, but that city made an equally poor impression on me when I had first arrived. I think another factor was the attitude of the Juventus people. They had pushed very hard and the pressure had come in an atmosphere that seemed to me to be verging on hysteria. Nor did I like the look of the Italian press. I have always got on well with the press in England. I don't mind criticism and I admire reporters who go about their work in a tough manner and ask good questions. In Manchester I used to have a running battle with the Daily Mail's top Soccer man in the north, Ron Crowther. He was always at me. I never lost my respect for the man. He knew his business. But the Italians seemed to be something else, and they seemed to carry unhealthy power.

I told Juventus that the first man to know my decision would be Albert Alexander, the Manchester City chairman. When I flew back to Manchester I hadn't made any comment about which way I was going. But I knew in my own mind that the dream was over. I had been in Italy 10 days and some Italian reporters wrote that I had been stringing the club along and enjoying a free holiday. They claimed I had never had any intention of leaving City. I would say that I always knew it would take a lot to get me to Juventus, but there were moments when I came within an inch of saying yes.

Those moments came when I thought of the scope of Juventus, the backing I would receive if I did any sort of a job. These people were ready to buy their way to glory and I thought that with my knowledge, my belief in a certain way of playing football, I could make a really big impact. Italy cried out for somebody to take hold of their football and make it live. The talent, the enthusiasm, and vast resources were there. All it needed was a man with the courage and the vision to harness these assets. I did think seriously that I might be that man. Down the last few years I have often re-examined my decision and wondered whether I lacked courage at a vital moment.

I honestly don't believe this was so. Ultimately, the strongest impulse that summer was to complete a job with Manchester City. We had won the championship and the FA Cup with a lot of style: we had matured very swiftly into a major team, and I wanted to know where could we go from there. That coming season we added the League Cup and the Cup-Winners Cup to our honours which, when you include the Second Division championship, meant that we had won five trophies in five years. In terms of titles won we had outstripped even Leeds United and Liverpool. Manchester United, our legendary rivals, had been left floundering.

It is wrong to pretend that what followed at Manchester City justified my Juventus decision. I never got the fulfilment I had hoped for. There was a taste of bitterness when I finally drove away from Maine Road.

But then it also is a fact that the man Juventus appointed

in the summer of 1969, a Czech, lasted just seven weeks.

## Chapter Nine

### The sediment of guilt

Of all the debts I owe to football perhaps the greatest is that it has taken me into every corner of the world. I've surfed off Bondi beach, been chased out of Mexico City with cries of 'Gringo Bandito' at my back, eaten lobster on San Francisco's Fisherman's Wharf, whiffed the magnolia blossom in Atlanta, and the great cities of Europe have become familiar to me. It is the great force of this game, this universal grip it has on the imagination of men. My own imagination had been stretched both by the game itself and the places it has taken me to. And nowhere more than in South Africa. It is a place of extraordinary beauty and grandeur. You feel that you are walking in a land of milk and honey. It is only slowly that you see, beneath all the riches, a harsh and terrible sadness.

That sadness, which comes to you like a chill wind once you emerge from the bastions of white society and encounter for the first time the reality of apartheid, was not apparent to me during the first of my two summers there. That summer, in 1972, was a time of gentle lotus eating. The directors of Cape Town City Football Club had invited me to organise six coaching 'clinics' in and around the city. It was rewarding work. Kids from all sections of

SOME OF THE COLOURS OF MY LIFE. Wembley before 100,000 fans, or Hackney Marshes before three ... football always draws me. Here are three sides that have a place in my life. (*Above*) my son, David – with cup – captain of his school team in 1967. (*Centre*) A Bunny club side in good shape before a charity match in 1973. (*Bottom*) A point of order during a training session for an MPs' side I coach.

*PA*                    *PA*

## CUP FEVER IN MY WEST HAM DAYS

Four days before we played Blackburn in the 4th Round, in 1956, we had a sea water bath at Hove. That's me on the right at the top. Recognise the other famous faces? Going down, they are John Bond, that prolific goalscorer John Dick, and Frank O'Farrell, who became Manchester United's manager. We won that match — and that's me leading out the team against Spurs in the next round.

Allison with his parents, Archie and Doris. The family background was always secure for Allison and his three brothers, Roy, Morris, Clive and his sister Pauline. He recalls "I was always proud of our semi-detached house in Bexleyheath. I never felt any pressures." Allison was born in Dartford and the family moved to Bexleyheath soon afterwards. The other Allison boys all now live in Canada. The father's death in 1974 at 65 hit Malcolm particularly hard. He says "My father's death came in the middle of a particularly hectic time at Crystal Palace. It was a shock and I deeply regretted that I had been unable to spend more time with him." Doris Allison still lives in Kent. She follows her son's turbulent career with a mixture of pride and resignation. Recently she insisted that he should change his hairstyle. He did so promptly.

THAT ITALIAN JOB   May 22 1969. London Airport. I had a four-year contract with Manchester City, but Juventus, the famous Italian club, were offering me £20,000 a year – plus a private plane – to manage the side. It was tempting – so, in lightweight suit and snazzy white shoes, I fly over to talk about it.

(*Opposite*) Relaxing on a ride round the Coliseum while I think over the offer. And (*inset*) a symbolic picture of what I did in the end: I threw the chance away. (*below*) Why I did. City were a great team ... and just ten months later I was at Wembley again, lifting the Football league cup after a 2-1 extra time win over West Bromwich Albion.

My Wembley Cup-winning smile says far more than any words

## DELIGHT AND DESPAIR
## WITH JOE MERCER

Two pictures that capture two contrasting
aspects of my relationship with my
Manchester City boss. On the left, we
bask in the adulation of cheering City fans
at Wembley, in 1969, after our 1-0 Cup
Final win over Leicester. I had to watch
the game from the stand because just six
months earlier, the FA had banned me
from sitting near the touchline for
swearing at a linesman. My expression
tells what I think of that verdict as I leave
the inquiry with Joe.

**THE PROMISE**  Joe Mercer and I, in the Manchester City stand, watch a build up in our own half ...

**THE EXCITEMENT**  A defence-splitting pass ... Franny is through ... surely he can put that one away ...

**THE DISAPPOINTMENT**  Oh dear! I'll have to talk to him about that one at half time ...

*Stewart Fraser*

Happy days with my family at our home in Manchester. From the left, my wife, daughter Dawn, aged 16, Michelle, aged six and Mark, 13. I have another son, David is not in the picture. He is living in Australia.

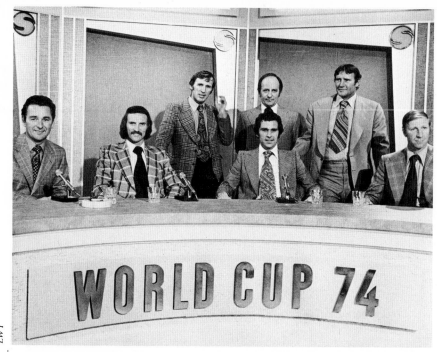

LWT

LINING UP BEFORE TWO DIFFERENT AUDIENCES, Brian Clough, Derek Dougan, Paddy Crerand, Brian Moore, Bobby Moncur, Jackie Charlton and myself pose for a different sort of camera during our appearances on the ITV World Cup panel. Below, one of the men who took a lot of stick from some members of that panel, Sir Alf Ramsey, joins Crystal Palace chairman Raymond Bloye and I in the directors' box for one of our home games. Recognise that pipe-smoking gentleman four rows behind? Yes, it's former ITV Head of Sport Jimmy Hill, now with BBC.

PA

## MY BIGGEST SIGNING

*PA*

London Airport. March 8, 1972. The trendy young man in the leather coat is Rodney Marsh. We are leaving for Manchester shortly after I had astonished the soccer world by buying him from Queen's Park Rangers for £200,000. I was slammed for buying this gifted ball wizard, but the move paid off for both of us.

May I introduce Miss Serena Williams.

Serena and I met when I was manager of Plymouth Argyle. We now live together in London.

Serena goes to most events with me ... whether it's a casual charity football match, or a top hat and tails Ascot meeting.

London News Service

Dave Willis

PA

MORE COLOURS OF MY LIFE. (*Top*) leaving a club with a friend. (*Left*) At a West End premiere. (*Right*) Shaking it at the Playboy.

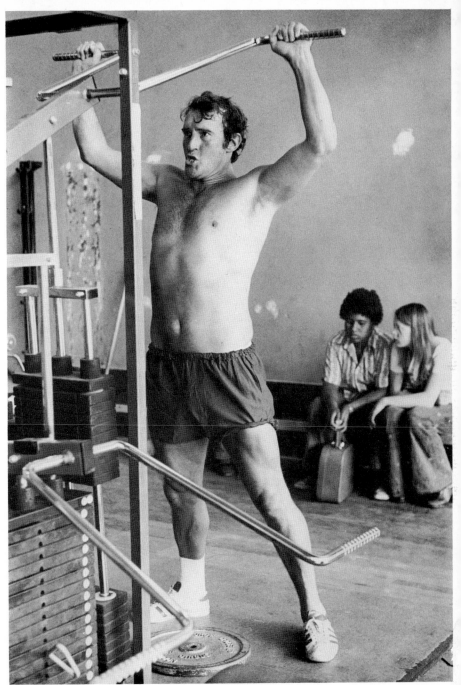

**THE MORNING AFTER THE NIGHT BEFORE** (or the morning before the night, whichever you want to look at it). Some might think you'd need to get in the gym pretty quickly to sweat out the champagne and cigar smoke after the nocturnal cavortings a few hours earlier. Others might think you have to put *in* some sweat in the morning to build up stamina to keep you going during those exertions. Certainly I've always believed in putting everything I've got into anything I do ... and these pictures seem to sum it all up.

A cigar … a glass … and time to ponder on all those colours of my life.

society were eager to learn, and I suppose at first the special hunger of the Cape coloureds and Africans was not so significant to me. And when the sessions were over I was able to relax in superb surroundings.

To sit on an old verandah on the slopes of Table Mountain, taking a glass of the good local wine, is to feel that you have found a very special corner of the world. I was staggered by the standard of living, and as the weeks rolled by I began to wonder if there was really any other way to spend one's life.

Back at Maine Road my seven-year partnership with Joe Mercer, which had been strained and creaking for more than a year, was finally splitting apart. The directors had driven a wedge between us. It was a sad and stupid business and when Coventry City came to Mercer with a job he decided to move on. There were one or two newspaper calls from London and Manchester attempting to get my reaction. But I didn't want to get involved. I had said all I wanted to Joe and the directors. I poured myself another glass of wine, happy to be so far away from all that nonsense. It was enough to let this gracious life style lap around me, smoothing away the accumulated pettiness of the previous nine months.

In 1973 I was invited back by the Cape Town directors. I was also asked to assemble those British footballers who were on summer engagements with South African clubs into a team for a series of 'Test' matches with select sides. There was much talent at my disposal, men like Frank McLintock, Rodney Marsh, Don Rogers, and the veteran Johnny Haynes. When I agreed to take on the team I didn't realise how much trouble and abuse I would be letting myself in for. I didn't suspect that the South African sports press—a strangely vicious and not very professional body of men—would inflate the matches in a series of needle games. Nor that they would hammer out stories which had no basis in fact.

We were accused of holding all-night parties on the eve

of games. Sir Stanley Matthews, who is earning some sort of living out there coaching coloured youngsters, was wheeled in to say that he was 'ashamed' of British football after our first game in Johannesburg. No doubt I had bought a few bottles of champagne, but the campaign against us was a travesty of the truth. The 'all night party' in fact was no more than a very sober visit to a millionaire's home on the outskirts of Johannesburg. It was a magnificent place, with a heated swimming pool and a snooker hall in the garden. Some of the boys had a few games of snooker. Our host ran a film. We were all back in our hotel by 11.30.

The problem was that we lost our first game in Johannesburg. A South African select beat us 3-2. We had not had time to adjust properly to the 6,000 ft. altitude, Rodney Marsh and Don Rodgers were some way from full fitness, and the referee was a beauty. The press murdered us. We were holidaymakers, philanderers. We insulted South African sport. Shamed England football. It was hysterical stuff, and no one had time to mention that the extraordinary referee had virtually wiped away our chances.

But the result was that the South Africans suddenly had some very angry and very talented players on their hands. We went to Durban and toyed with the South Africans, winning 4-1. At Cape Town we cruised to another win, this by 3-0. And all the time we were relishing the thoughts of returning to Johannesburg. We won the final 'Test' 3-1. The coloured and African supporters gave us tremendous cheers. It had all become very serious.

But for all of us those matches against white South Africa paled against an extraordinary afternoon in Johannesburg's shanty town.

We had agreed to play a coloured team in the Orlando Stadium. When we got to the stadium the atmosphere was incredible. There were hundreds of white police around the stadium. They had with them the fiercest-looking alsatians I have ever seen. The coloured fans, who made an amiable comparison with some of the morons who find their way into our own football grounds, were searched thoroughly and roughly before they went through the turnstiles. For some of us it was our first glimpse of that other side of South Africa.

Twenty-three thousand fans packed into the stadium and they had plenty to cheer about. Their team were marvellous, full of adventure and skill. They would have taken the 1974 World Cup team Zaire apart. We beat them, but it was a desperate struggle. A South American coach had got hold of them and given them some rudimentary organisation. But out of this very basic team plan there sprang some astonishingly free football. Their players were known by nicknames and their star player, a brilliant individualist, was called 'the cardshuffler'. Certainly he shuffled the ball with great and apparently unending skill. Once three of our defenders, including that terrific reader of a defensive situation, McLintock, attempted to block him out on the touch-line. 'Cardshuffler' simply sent each one in a different direction.

Throughout the game the fans were an integral part. Their enthusiasm, their eagerness to see skill, transmitted itself to the players and Don Rogers and Rodney Marsh also did much to reward them for paying out £1 a head for their tickets.

Later in our hotel there was an apparently historic scene. The coloured team and their officials came up to talk to us about the game over a few drinks. The British Ambassador came along. But the Secretary of the South African Football Association refused to attend. The coloureds were so eager for information, for knowledge to improve themselves. You sensed so strongly in them their feeling of isolation and now, this evening, the gates had opened to them. You were conscious too that those gates would slam again the moment we left the place. It was as though they were trying to horde every minute against the future.

Apart from the alsatians, and some thick, leather whips, the suggestions of apartheid that day were relatively subdued. Indeed, as I had learned the previous summer, it is possible to visit South Africa and totally miss the implications and weight of the racial policy.

But when you have played a match against skilled and brave opponents, seen those opponents express themselves at times with great brilliance, and then realise that once the final whistle has gone they are no longer your equals, it has a great impact.

I do not know the politics of South Africa beyond the fact that the whites have a tremendous vested interest in preserving a way of life which is rich beyond most Englishmen's dreams; and that they see the coloured population as a great threat to that way of life. I suppose it is not courteous for a visitor to tell his hosts how they should run their country. I suppose the answer is not to visit that country. But do we leave those coloured footballers in isolation?

Towards the end of our tour we were in Durban at carnival time. After training McLintock, Marsh, Haynes, and myself used to take a drink in a rather smart bar. One evening three Africans were making very good music outside on the pavement. Without thinking, I called them in. I suppose it was a thoughtless thing to do. The barmen raged. One or two of the customers were also appalled. The barman roared at me: "Do you want me to lose my job?"

Of course it is easy to hold up your hands and say this is disgusting. But I accept that many of the whites probably feel, in their way, as trapped as the the coloureds. Certainly they hunger for contact from outside. Their passion for sport is their one obvious outlet.

My hope is that sport can play a role, however marginally, in the ending of this great country's isolation. I hope so for all those wonderfully alive people in the shanty town stadium in Johannesburg. And also for all those white people whose decent instincts are held on tight rein by a harsh political reality.

Certainly it would be nice to take again a glass of wine on the slopes of Table Mountain. Without tasting the sediment of guilt.

# Chapter Ten

## The quality of Mercer

When Joe Mercer and I were friends no-one in football could live with us. Between us we had it all. I charged into situations like a bull, full of aggressive ambition and a contempt for anyone who might be standing in my way. And Joe came behind me, picking up pieces, soothing the wounded and the offended with that vast charm which touched and affected all those who came in contact. He was the boss, he had the controlling voice, but he recognised that I was making things happen for him. The first time I met him I knew he was a star, a man who had been given so much more than the natural ability which it takes to become a merely famous footballer. There was a puckish humour which cut through the pompous like a knife stroke. There were biting, colourful phrases which rolled off his tongue on their way from a great fund of shrewdness and knowledge of life. He bailed me out of trouble so many times. He was a father figure and a partner, and he knew my value.

So why is it that I no longer care, one way or the other, whether I hear from Joe Mercer again? How is it that the memory of those brilliant years, when we took on the might and legend of Matt Busby and Manchester United and won, has curdled and soured? It is a long and not unpainful story and the seed of it was sown on Manchester City's team coach travelling to our First League match at Middlesbrough. Mercer sat beside me and as the miles ticked by we discussed all our plans, the players we needed, our style of play, and finally he said: "Son, if you do well with City ·there will be great rewards. Two years will do me."

I know now that in some crucial ways my thinking then was naive. I suspect that Mercer exploited this in an instinctive sort of way. He knew that I had one overwhelming ambition. That was to build a great side, to make my mark in a way that he had done in his playing days at Everton and Arsenal. He had become an aristocrat out on the field in the colours of two famous clubs and in the white shirt of England. I still had to make my push. Mercer had recognised that I might have something a bit unique inside me, but I remained a nonentity in the game. No one really knew me. But they couldn't put me down once I became Joe Mercer's man.

It was very impressive to see the way Joe moved about the game. Everyone knew him. And they all liked him. At first his nerves were still shaky. He had had a bad time at Aston Villa and it had left him drawn and ill. But as Manchester City's health strengthened so too did Joe's. He quickly lost the one attitude to the game which had disappointed me when I first met him. He had initially been obsessed with aggressive play, possibly because of his failure at Aston Villa. I say failure even though he would claim that he produced a lot of good players for that club. But in the strict terms of results he did not succeed, and this left him with something of a tactical hangover. He wanted to stress Manchester City's power. I told him that in my opinion he had got the game out of context, especially with his own deep instincts for good, cultured football.

But it was only a temporary disagreement. As soon as he saw that the team was improving, that we were getting

103

shape and purpose, he began to relax. He got back a good sense of priorities. And Joe's lapse, given his experiences, was commendably brief. Don Revie, another gifted, natural player had a much longer flirtation with physical power play, and of course it was Sir Alf Ramsey's most consistent contribution to our national team. He elevated power beyond skill, we won the World Cup with a good side which had some very ordinary players, and we are still suffering.

Joe taught me many things. He knew how to conserve himself and though he had one or two bad days, he usually came into the ground very fresh and very alive. We won the Second Division, we steadied ourselves in the First Division, and then we swept through to a brilliant championship win in 1968. Our football flowed in exciting, fluid patterns, and Joe summed up beautifully our last push to the title. We had to win our last two games, at Spurs and Newcastle. He said: "Now we have got to climb Everest and K2 in a week, but we can do it."

Our partnership, which had developed into a great personal friendship, reached a sort of perfection in that championship year. Joe tolerated my excesses, my indiscreet lifestyle, and once when I went to him and said: "Joe, I'm in a bit of trouble, I need £134," he put his hand in his pocket and gave me the cash. He had strict rules about lending money, even though he was very generous with some of his old playing colleagues. He used to tell me that I was foolish with my money, that I was easily exploited by people. He may have had something. But I also argued that certainly people took advantage of him. He helped his old colleague Tommy Lawton a lot, and I did say that I felt Lawton wasn't giving too much back. But Joe wasn't a fool. He set a limit on the amount of money he would lend out at any one time.

If there was any friction between us in that first five years it was because I felt Joe tended to defer to the directors too much. Perhaps it was his background as a miner's son, but he did seem to have an excessive respect for the establishment. He didn't believe that you could take them on and win. And this annoyed me when we were in a position of such strength. We had taken the club up from nothing, money was pouring into the club, and yet sometimes I would go to Joe and say: "Look, we must sort out this or that player's contract," and he would drag his feet because he didn't want to upset the directors. Sometimes it seemed to me that Joe wanted power and success, but he also wanted a happy, contented life without too much strife. He wasn't eager to go battling in the boardroom.

But I don't want to stress this aspect. It was something very much in the margins, completely overshadowed by his tremendous presence. I worked closely with the team, firing them, pressing them, and when Joe and I talked we were almost invariably on the same wavelength. Once he over-ruled me on a team decision at Stoke. I wanted to convert Mike Summerbee to centre forward, and I had even told the players. But Joe said no. As it happened, we lost 3-0 and as I walked up the tunnel towards the dressing rooms I felt very bitter. A supporter shouted "Allison" and as I turned to look he spat in my face and said "You will drag the club down, Allison." If I could have got at him I would have torn him apart. I felt so frustrated. I was bitter with Joe. But he smoothed it over—and the following Saturday Mike Summerbee was at centre forward.

In fact Mercer's feeling for tactics and the shape of a team was remarkably sharp. And he was very good at passing on to me things he had learned from life. One of his favourite sayings was: "Mal, always celebrate your victories." He also quoted me Stanley Baldwin when we wrestled with one team decision. We were going down to play a Cup replay at Ipswich. On the Saturday our full back Bobby Kennedy had had a terrible game. I couldn't make my mind about him. Joe said: "When in doubt do nowt." We didn't, Bobby Kennedy completely recovered his game, and we won comfortably.

I got to love Joe, his touches of wisdom, his ability to attack all sorts of problems with a flash of humour, and the protection he offered me in sudden storms. The strength of the relationship was that it was perfectly balanced in every respect. I had the physical strength to go out on the training pitch to drive players harder than ever before, to push them into corners from which they had to come out better players. And when they were low Joe would reassure them, flatter them a bit.

We carried the FA Cup in the spring of 1969, and again Joe told me that my future as manager of Manchester City was assured. We made a poor start to season 69/70, but after Christmas we found ourselves poised for more glory. We knocked Manchester United out of the League Cup semi-finals, and we were among the favourites to win the European Cup-Winners Cup. Joe said to me: "This year will do me, Mal." It was nearly five years since Joe had made a similar remark on the team coach travelling to Middlesbrough. But the times had been so good, so rich, and fulfilling, that I had never pressed the point. I had a pang of jealousy at Wembley on Cup Final day when Joe walked out with the team. I thought: "I should be there, too." But I still felt confident that he would, sooner or later, organise a neat transfer of power. I felt he would look after me.

I understand things a lot more clearly now. I understand that when a man has become accustomed to glory and to success he is reluctant to face the day when he has to bow out. This must be especially so when that man knows he has somebody working for him who can help him so much in guaranteeing success. Sir Matt Busby once said to me: "If I had you working for me I would be a manager until I was 70." Perhaps Joe had a similar feeling. I don't blame him for his attitude. Success is like a drug. And we had both become mainliners. If I had known those things then I would have disregarded Joe's assurances about the future and our relationship would not have come under such strain. We might still be working together at Maine Road.

The whole experience has taught me never to make promises to any man who works for me. I will never say that I will step aside. It is something I believe that a man can never really say because he can never be sure how he will feel tomorrow. Perhaps Joe Mercer wasn't to know this. He had never come up fighting as a manager or coach. When his playing career was over he naturally moved into management. People knew him, recognised him as a big man in the game. So I accept that he probably didn't quite realise the depth of my ambitions as we moved into the spring of 1970. As we sat in a rain storm at the Prater Stadium, Vienna, watching our team beat the Poles of Gornik for the Cup-Winners Cup trophy, I thought that my time had come. We had towels over our heads, the rain slanted in cold on our faces, but it was a warm feeling that spread through my body. I had slogged for five years and now I was to receive real status. I didn't want to clamber over Joe. I wanted recognition of my work with the team. I wanted to be team manager. Joe could have any title he wanted.

I still valued him highly and I imagined we could work together as closely as before. But now I was to get the acceptance of a manager in my own right. It was a good feeling I took back to the old, luxurious hotel near the Hapsburg's palace. Harry Godwin, City's witty and tremendously conscientious chief scout, played the piano right through to dawn. Francis Lee danced on top of the piano—in his underpants. And in the morning we kept the plane waiting at Vienna airport. We got another Civic Reception at Manchester Town Hall—our fourth in three years. We were outpacing the giants of English football, Leeds, Liverpool, and of course, Manchester United. And I was to lead City towards fresh triumphs. Only I wasn't. Slowly it dawned on me that Joe was again drawing a veil over his commitments to me. He threw me a sprat. I could be called team manager, but he would still make the final decisions. I realised, bitterly, that Joe was hanging on.

I suppose it was then I decided to organise a take-over of Manchester City.

Apart from my impatience over status, I was not satisfied with the way the club was being run. I felt the club had become big, but that the people in control in the boardroom had not grown with it.

I liked and admired Albert Alexander, the little, twinkling Chairman, but some of the people around him staggered me with their lack of vision. The former secretary Walter Griffiths and I were often in dispute and the board would back him on small administrative matters, like the size of hotel bills. I used to think to myself, "What is all this, I've helped lift this club from the grave and now I get this sort of treatment."

I knew that the City Vice-Chairman Frank Johnson was ready to sell a huge chunk of shares for £100,000 and that the man who bought them had only to make one or two available alliances and he would win control of the club. So I said to Ian Niven, a fanatical City supporter who is now on the board: "Find me a man with £100,000, and we will get control of the club." Niven came up with the man within a fortnight, Joe Smith, a double-glazing 'tycoon' from Oldham. I had had enough of being patted on the head. I thought that if I was not going to be given what was my due, I would attempt to take it for myself. I met Joe Smith out at his home in the Cheshire countryside. He told me how, as a penniless youth, he had climbed over the wall at Maine Road to watch football. He was ready to do all he could to develop Manchester City. He wanted to give me a 20-year contract. I was apparently in business.

Actually, I had been talking in 'peanuts' when I mentioned the figure of £100,000 to Ian Niven. I learned later that around a great industrial and commerical town like Manchester there was scores of wealthy men ready to buy into the most successful club in English football. I got my first hint that the take-over was not going to be the smooth, 'big-time' operation I imagined when I heard that Smith and Johnson were haggling over the price of the controlling shares. Johnson wanted £110, 000, Smith was offering £100,000. And in the middle of their haggle I was told about a man called Ralph Levy. He was a rainwear manufacturer who was ready to come in with £500,000.

I went to see Levy and we got on well. Yes, he wanted to buy into City. He would immediately put in £500,000. I could see Manchester City taking off. But even as we were talking Joe Smith was finally agreeing a price with Johnson. Levy had come in too late. However he wasn't dismayed. He said: "Malcolm, is there another football club we might buy?" I told him that I had heard that control of Bolton Wanderers could be bought for £50,000. He was interested. He said that he would buy control of Bolton, make me manager and also a director of one of his companies, and that I would become the best paid man in football.

It was a tempting thought, but Bolton was a run-down club and I was reluctant to face so quickly the sort of operation I had just completed with Manchester City. I had built a brilliant team at City and I was enjoying too much the satisfaction which had come with that work.

And Joe Smith, having got over the £10,000 wrangle—he had agreed to pay the extra—was full of promises. I would have this incredible contract. I would be given control of the team, though there would be an important place, always, at the club for Joe Mercer. It was a time for me to take a low profile within the club, for the directors were fighting the Smith take-over legally. They claimed that Johnson had broken a 'covenant' not to sell the shares without first offering them to current members of the board. And when I returned from a few days in London I heard that the board were meeting on the Friday evening and that afterwards, according to Alexander, there was likely to be a "sensational" statement. I learned that that statement, almost certainly, would be about the sacking of Malcolm Allison. Apparently the board had gone to Joe Mercer as soon as they heard the news of Smith's share purchase—a front page splash in the Daily Express—and asked him: "Whose side are you on?" Joe had said that he was with them, adding in that silvery way: "How do you hi-jack a football club in full flight?"

I took the players for a short training session on the Friday afternoon before the board meeting. We were due to play Leeds United at Leeds the following day. The players were a little hostile towards me. Francis Lee, Mike Summerbee, and Colin Bell came to me and said: "Why try to change the club, Malcolm? We have done well. You do not change something that works." I think Lee and Summerbee learned eventually the strength of my thinking. But at that time I was very much out on a limb. Joe Mercer came out onto the pitch and said that the directors wanted to see me. As we walked back towards the boardroom, Joe said to me: "You are on your own now, Malcolm." When he said that to me I knew that the relationship had gone. I turned to him and said: "That doesn't bother me, Joe. I've always been on my own. I know that." The directors quizzed me, asked me where I stood in the affair. I said I was only interested in the future of Manchester City. I felt we were on the verge of being a truly great club, but that the penny-pinching, small-time attitude of the board had depressed me. It was all very cool. I sensed that I was on my way out.

On the team coach to Leeds on the Saturday morning Joe came to sit beside me. He had had a change of mind. He said to me: "Son, I have thought it over, and it is you and me together. We are this bloody club." But I couldn't warm to Joe that morning. His remark about me being on my own the previous evening had deadened a lot of feeling I had for him.

Manchester City sacked me at 6 o'clock. It happened in the corridor of the Leeds United ground. The Chairman,

Alexander, gave me the news. He said: "Malcolm, the board want to sack you." I liked the little guy and I knew this was a painful business for him. I put my arm around him—he was only 5 feet 2 inches and said: "Albert, we have always had a good association, you do what you feel you have to." As I spoke, Joe Mercer joined us. His expression was very intense. He said to the Chairman: "If he goes, I go." Joe had confirmed his position of the morning—and he won me a reprieve.

They returned to the Leeds boardroom. A few minutes later I was asked to meet four directors at the Piccadilly Hotel in Manchester. At the hotel I had another cool meeting with the directors. But I was reinstated, even though it was clear that the only reason was that Mercer had insisted that he would also leave. Even so, I felt a break had come between Joe and myself. I sensed that the best of our relationship had gone. Twice he had made big promises about power coming over to me at a certain time. And these had been specific promises.

I had never made great demands on him and I had now reached the conclusion that Joe had been basically looking after himself. Joe's "It's you and me together" statement on the way to Leeds had propped up our partnership. But it had come too late to ultimately save it.

The new board, which contained Joe Smith and his allies Ian Niven and Simon Cussins, failed to please either of us. Joe Smith asked me what I wanted. I said I wanted a good contract and that I wanted to be boss. Mercer said that I should be made team manager, but that he should continue to have the final say. I was terribly disillusioned with Joe Smith when I saw my new contract. It was full of loopholes. My solicitor spent several months working on it and still it wasn't right. I remember saying to the directors: "My contract isn't worth a light."

Bad feelings were beginning to replace the drive and thrust which had carried me—and City—into such a position of strength in the game. I felt terribly frustrated. I couldn't put my mind to the job. And Joe and I were no longer intimates. We had begun to drift apart and there were moments, for the first time, of real hostility between us. I recall a row in a hotel bar in Malta. It started off as a converstion about power and men and there were other people in the talk. But the subject was too close to the bone for Joe and me. I got heated. I contrast that with an earlier trip we made together shortly before our Cup-Winner Cup success. We went to Portugal, travelling up from Lisbon to the University town of Coimbra by train. We had drawn the local team Academica in the quarter-finals of the competition. We had had a few drinks in one of the great squares of Lisbon before getting on to the train and we were both a little tipsy when we arrived at the up-country railway station. We were not really prepared for an imposing reception committee waiting on the platform. It was a warm, friendly trip. We went to check on the team hotel at Bussaco, scene of one of Wellington's great battles. And our swords stayed in their scabbards.

For what was there to fight about? We were on course again for two more major trophies. Joe had brought a marvellous flourish to a managerial career which had once threatened to fall below the level of his playing days. He had nourished my ability as a coach. Where before I had been banging on doors with a terrible, angry impatience, Joe had strooled along, bow-leggedly, with a key. If ever two men had gained from joining forces they were Joe and I.

The break had come when I realised that Joe was keeping hold of that key. That became increasingly clear in the new season, and when I fell foul of the authorities again—and was banned for two months—there was a terrible row.

We had to play three games over the Easter programme, and then meet Chelsea in the semi-final of the Cup-Winners Cup. I was officially out of the game so I could advise Joe only from a distance, but I felt sure that he would realise the impossibility of asking players to get

112

through four games in six days, the last match being absolutely vital to the club's hopes of winning five trophies in four years. City lost the first two games of the programme, against Nottingham Forest and Huddersfield. And this prompted Joe to do an incredible thing. He played the full team again at Newcastle—two days before the big Cup tie, again with Chelsea. I couldn't believe it. I was very angry. I said that Joe was on some sort of ego trip, tht he couldn't stand to lose three straight matches while he was in sole charge of the team, and this had completely clouded his judgment.

The news from Newcastle confirmed my worst fears. Colin Bell, Mike Doyle, and Joe Corrigan had all been badly injured. The team had been wrecked 48 hours before a game which would determine our season. I rang Joe and what I said to him on that call more or less wrecked any hopes of restoring our partnership. I told him he was full of ego, which I suppose was a remarkable statement coming from me.

What happened afterward was no more than a series of pinpricks. We couldn't agree on the signing of Rodney Marsh. I did a deal with Queen's Park Rangers for £140,000 and Joe advised the board not to pay the VAT involved, so it fell through. When the deal finally went through it cost us £200,000. I had agreed £180,000 with Jim Gregory, the Rangers Chairman, but he only needed 10 minutes with Joe Smith and another director, Eric Alexander, to push that up by another £20,000. And when Rodney arrived, admittedly some way from full fitness, Joe Mercer sniped away. By then I had assumed full control of management decisions, but Joe Mercer was a sort of shadowy presence. We couldn't get close any more and when Coventry City invited him to go as general manager with Gordon Milne he made a quick decision. I was in South Africa at the time, but I gather that he had stage managed the move beautifully. Manchester City, and I, received a lot of bad publicity. Right to the end, it seemed

113

to me, Joe had controlled his personal position with great skill. He had come out smelling of roses.

It would be nice to say that the intervening years have softened the raw feelings. But if I am honest I have to say that this hasn't happened. What should be a great friendship, an alliance between different but very compatible men, is broken. Joe Mercer, reviewing the period we had spent together before the bad time came, once said to me: "Mal, these have been the best five years of my life. I wouldn't have traded them for anything." I felt the same way. And I could never regret working with Joe Mercer. It was an education in life and in ambition.

I suppose the best thing to say is that there is nothing owing from that relationship. We gained so much from it personally, though in the process we lost the thing which made all those successes happen, an implicit friendship and understanding. My complaint, my bitterness, flows from a feeling that the relationship was always tilted subtly in Joe's favour. I cannot feel that he had any appreciation of my situation. That was the thing that got me in the end.

And yet I do not blame Joe Mercer. In so many ways he is a brilliant man. I thought his brief, caretaker role as England manager in the summer of 1974 was carried off with all the panache and the style I have come to associate with him.

I think Joe might have been tempted to take me along with him on that England run. But as I have suggested he is a man of great pride. We talked for an hour at the Football Writers Dinner, shortly before he took over the England team. We can still communicate, but a vital element has gone.

Perhaps it has little to do with Joe Mercer, and more to do with the game, which makes men think first of all in terms of survival. Joe came from the old school, and he learned those lessons of survival well. I came from a different, more reckless school. And ultimately, I suspect, that was the difference between us. I regret it deeply, but it is a fact. And one of the saddest ones.

# Chapter Eleven

## The birth of a team

Manchester United, the best-loved team in England, quickly became an object of hatred to me when I moved into the city. I loathed the bumptious, patronising tones of some of their players, their hangers-on, and many of their supporters. It became a challenge to me when I drove past city parks and saw perhaps 20 youngsters playing football, with at least ninety per cent of them wearing the famour red shirts of United. I felt a flush of anger when my son Mark got involved in a fight on his first day at a new school. An older boy had said to him, "Hey, Allison, foureyes, I want to see you after school. Your dad works for that useless team City." Mark didn't wait for the school bell. He walked over to the United boy and gave him a whack. That's how I felt. I wanted to punish these United people who believed that there could only be one team in the city.

I had been in the town only a few days when I found myself at United's championship dinner. Sir Matt Busby, in the course of his speech, turned and said: "I believe there is room for two First Division clubs in Manchester." And I thought to myself, "Yes, baby, and you're going to get two teams." Later Sandy Busby, Sir Matt's son, and some friends were coming over very strongly about United's deeds, their strength, and how it was impossible for City to seriously challenge them. I said: "Your father has got a 20-year start, but I'll pass him in three." Now that was a bad thing to say. But a very good thing to think.

I had got into a very angry mood at that dinner. There was so much self-satisfaction in the air. Even Vic Bernard, the chairman of Stockport County, was giving me a bad time. We were talking at the bar and my friends Noel Cantwell and Maurice Setters were also in the company. Bernard, who had just taken over Stockport, said that he had considered me for his manager's job, and then outlined his programme. Stockport would immediately be promoted to the Third Division, then the Second, and, perhaps after a season of consolidation, it would be the top flight. I said to Cantwell and Setters, "I think we had better push off before he wins the European Cup."

I suppose that when I went to Maine Road for my interview in the summer of 1965, my attitude to life was unusual. I was dressed casually, a fawn suit with an open-necked blue shirt, and I had been talking with the directors—who seemed a very elderly set of men—only a few minutes when I said, "Look, gentlemen, you don't know me and I don't know you. I'll work for you until Christmas for £30 a week. Then we will have another talk." It was quite a generous gesture on my part. But I wanted to work for Manchester City. Joe Mercer had shown faith in me. Since my boyhood Manchester City always had had for me a magical ring to its name. They agreed to the proposition and I started work immediately. I was very positive, very keen to get into the Manchester United crowd. Their feeling that they were the greatest things that ever walked had really got inside me.

There was clearly, though, a mountain of work to do. But that wasn't a novel experience. Each time I had moved, from Cambridge to Bath, from Bath to Plymouth, I had felt I was leaving a better side. And again I felt it with

Manchester. I sat with Joe Mercer and watched our first game, a friendly match with Dundee United at Maine Road. We lost 2-1 and we were both very shocked. "What a terrible team", I recall groaning.

The atmosphere at the place was appalling. People who didn't cheat, were hiding, their confidence shattered. Alan Oakes, who emerged as one of the best midfield and defensive players in the League and came close to winning an England cap, used to break out in a sweat before a game. No one had got through to him and told him how well he could play. I could understand how it was that angry fans had stoned the ground the previous season. Joe and I had walked into a mausoleum. There was a friendly game at Tranmere, which gave us no more comfort. Catching Manchester United, it seemed, was going to be a marathon run. But we tinkered about. We tried different things in training, we were concerned to patch up our deficiencies.

It was crucial to get something out of our first League match, at Middlesbrough. I had noticed in training the good running ability and toughness of a boy called David Connor. I thought that he had potential to be a valuable defensive player, a man perhaps to shut out the opposing play-maker. In Middlesbrough's case, that was Ian Gibson, a very good and subtle player. Connor, who was full of stamina, achieved the shut-out. Gibson never really got going and we came away with a draw. It was a good, solid start, and very important in terms of building early confidence. We went eight games without defeat. We were 'nicking' a few results, but it all helped.

You have to understand the demoralisation that had gripped this team. Just a few miles across the city was Old Trafford, a sort of momument of reproach to all the City boys. They were chopping blocks, clowns. The 'team' was United. United player Pat Crerand had bet me £10 that we would never again get 30,000 fans into our ground. Not too many people would have taken him on. But the early results came like a little, freshening breeze. We might just have a chance. Neil Young was showing to me that beneath an often timid approach there was a marvellously delicate skill and thunderous shooting power.

Mike Doyle, a policeman's son, had a built-in aggression and Glyn Pardoe, who had struck me as a bit of a dumpling when I arrived, each day showed a little more of his class. I quickly cashed in on Doyle's aggression, ordering him to interchange with the centre forward in bursts during games. His runs into the box from midfield had an element of great surprise and though the ruse was quickly picked up by opponents it was a brilliant short-term success. Doyle got seven goals in a few games, giving us a vital thrust towards the top of the Second Division. Our chief problems were in defence. I suggested to Joe Mercer that we buy Everton's reserve centre half George Heslop. He agreed and it proved a crucial stroke. Heslop gave us a lot more polish at the back.

Joe Mercer had made two signings, one brilliant, one somewhat less so. Mike Summerbee instantly began to pay off his transfer fee. He came to us as a rather defensive winger but I refused to let him play in his own half. I made him more aggressive and the result was devastating. Joe also signed Ralph Brand, a move which worked out badly. Brand, a sensation in Scotland, had lots of skill but he didn't have the power to put it together consistently well enough for us. It was a sad thing to lose his skill, but we had to discard him.

I wanted to sign two players, Colin Bell and Wyn Davies, but we had only the money for one. I decided on Bell, but Joe wasn't sure. Also doubtful were most of the First Division managers. This gave me a chance; for our Directors were clucking about trying to raise money, £42,000 for him. I was telling people in the game that Bell couldn't play, hoping desperately that the board could get the money together in time. They did it with hours to spare. We signed him on the eve of the transfer deadline in March, 1966, beating off a late challenge by Blackpool

119

manager Ron Suart.

Bell's signing more or less guaranteed us the Second Division championship. It was a major triumph, unthinkable at the start of the season. But in a town which had become used to Manchester United sweeping to titles, it seemed to have little impact. That was dispiriting, but I had always known it would be a long, tough haul. More discouraging was the reaction of the board. The chairman, Albert Alexander, came to me and said, "Walter Griffiths, the secretary, is getting a bonus of £400, so are you, and Joe Mercer is getting £600." I was a bit stunned. Then I felt disgust. I felt I had been badly insulted.

I remember saying: "Yes, I thought the secretary did very well. He booked us into some very nice hotels."

I had worked up to Christmas on £30 a week as agreed. Then we had some talks and I got a £10-a-week rise. But really it was chickenfeed. I didn't have a club car or any other perks. I knew the club wasn't rolling in money, but this did seem very cheap. Eventually they agreed to pay off my overdraft which stood at £600. I hadn't been bowled over by their generosity.

But the work was going well and I persuaded Joe Mercer that we should sign my man Tony Book from Plymouth. Joe hadn't been too happy, stressing Book's age. But I asked him "Were you finished when you left Everton for Arsenal?" I also told him that I had watched eight other right full backs and not one of them had come near to Book in speed, control, and class. Joe was a bit uptight about it but he agreed and we gave Plymouth £16,000.

Just how well the money had been spent did not become clear until our first real crisis in the First Division. We started the season briskly enough and again confidence was growing. Then the roof fell in. We went to Villa and lost 3-0. West Ham murdered us 4-1, and Chelsea also had an easy 3-0 win. We had crumpled. The defence had simply caved in. It was now that the true value of Tony Book became apparent at Maine Road.

I changed the system of our play. Tony Book switched to the sweeping role, still a rarity in England, with the rest of the defence marking man for man. The improvement was immediate. We came out of our dive towards the foot of the table and in the sixth round of the FA Cup we nearly caused a sensation at Leeds. We lost 1-0. But we did outplay them. Colin Bell missed three chances, incredibly, and in every phase of the game we had an edge. The point was that we nearly caught Leeds with a sucker punch. I knew how thorough Leeds were, how Don Revie had people like Syd Owen analysing every aspect of an opponent's game. So I suggested we completely change our system. We went to play 4-2-4 and it nearly worked. We finished the season comfortably in mid-table and Harry Godwin, the chief scout, came up to me and said, "In the 13 seasons I've been at Maine Road, we have only been above the bottom six in the First Division four times." I felt we had made good progress. And our performance against Leeds had given me the first inkling that we could go on and reach out for the big prizes. The great disappointment of the season had been our performance at Old Trafford. All the old doubts and frailties came flooding back once the team got to Manchester United's ground. We put on a terribly limp performance and I was disgusted for days. We had been cuffed aside by the giants again.

Yet we did go into season 67-68 thinking that we had got a bit of a chance. I had persuaded Joe Mercer to sign Tony Coleman from Doncaster Rovers and when I did it I knew I was taking a tremendous gamble.

Tony Coleman's record read like the nightmare of a delirious probation officer. A brilliant young player, he had been thrown out of Stoke City and Preston North End and described as 'unmanageable'. He drifted into non-league football with Bangor City in North Wales, and then Doncaster Rovers tempted him back into the league. There he promptly flattened a referee with a punch in the face. Joe Mercer didn't really want to know when I proposed we

121

bought him from Bangor. Joe was friendly with the Bangor manager, Tommy Jones, the former Everton player, and had been told to forget it. But we could have had him for £3,000 from Bangor. I thought it was worth the risk. At Doncaster the asking price was £12,000. But it still seemed cheap one night when I saw him totally dominate a game. He was so strong along the left. And we needed a left winger to give us width and balance. Mercer, with a resigned expression on his face, said: "Go on then. Give it a go."

Ultimately, I failed with Tony Coleman. I did get two superb years out of him. He was a crucial element in our First Division championship and FA Cup wins. But I could never deal fully with the strange, wild streak in him. There was something in him that no one could get to. I remember vividly a training session shortly before the Cup final. I said to him: "Come on Tony, you can give it more than that." And he sort of sneered, saying: "What's the point?" The point was that he was on a bonus of £1,500 to win the next match.

I wanted to swipe his choirboy face. And eventually I did that. I had placed a midnight curfew on him. Generally he did behave himself and his face used to break into a cherubic smile when I used to compliment him on his performances in training. He had an incredible strength and this made it difficult to decide if he had been out on the tiles. You only have to look at most players to decide how much sleep they have had. But it was almost impossible with Coleman. Anyway, I got a tip that he was out after midnight in a nightclub in Manchester. He was with Ken Mulhearn, another Liverpool boy who I had bought from Stockport County. He had nice, clean hands and was nearly a very good goalkeeper. I drove straight to the Cabaret club and there was Coleman smiling away at the end of the bar. I slapped him across the face. It wasn't a punch, but it did express my anger and disappointment. This was a kid who had been given a chance he had no right to expect.

Coleman wanted to make a full scale fight of it. I got him out of the nightclub. However I decided he probably had to go. The team was moving so well, I just couldn't afford to let anyone get away with it.

But as we moved into that season of 67-68 I knew Coleman was going to be a terrific force. He was a driving, hustling sort of player and he also had much skill. I also wanted Francis Lee, a player of even greater potential.

Lee was the slightly strutting, blonde-haired emperor of Bolton Wanderers. I loved the swagger and aggression in his play. It was so much more than mere cockiness. Joe Mercer and I went to see him play against Liverpool and any doubts that he could make it at the top vanished for both of us. I felt he was my kind of guy. I went to see him after one game and I said: "If I had you I would make you a great player." Apparently, when I left the room he said: "What an arrogant bastard. He can make me a great player." Stoke City's Tony Waddington also wanted him badly. But Francis chose Manchester City and with that decision I knew that we had the equipment to go right to the top.

Franny was the extra dimension we needed. His aggression and confidence lifted some of the pressure from Summerbee, who in this department had been carrying something of a lone burden.

I first got the taste of a championship victory in a home match with Nottingham Forest. The previous season they had promised to emerge as a major force, finishing League runners-up and FA Cup semi-finalists. I had a boy called Paul Hince on the right wing. I had him picked up from local amateur football. He had a superb game against the big Forest full back, Winfield. He tortured him, and when the back began to make some outrageous fouls, I roared to the ref: "Get that man off the field." Hince, who was a bright boy and now works in sports journalism, got off the floor gamely and shouted to me: "Don't get him sent off, Mal, I might not be able to beat the next man they put on me." Hince slaughtered Winfield, Summerbee adjusted beautifully to the role of centre forward, and we won 2-0. I knew we had real chances now.

Peter Doherty, one of the men I admire most in football, and my racing friend Arthur Shaw came to watch an FA Cup replay we were involved in at Reading. We had been embarrassed on our own ground by the Third Division side and we attacked the replay in a ruthless mood. We won 7-0 and as the teams left the pitch the man on the loudspeaker said: "Ladies and gentlemen, you have just seen one of the greatest teams England has produced in a long time." That might have been a slightly biased view in that he had just seen his own side taken apart. But Doherty said: "That was quite a brilliant performance." And Arthur Shaw, who had drifted away from the game since his Arsenal playing days, told me that his interest in the game had been revived. He became a Manchester City supporter and predicted that five of our players would win England caps.

We were developing so quickly that I was unprepared for defeat in a later Cup replay at Leicester. We led 2-0 after 20 minutes, but our goalkeeper, Ken Mulhearn made some bad mistakes and we lost 4-3. It took a stunning victory at Old Trafford to finally dispel that depression. The Manchester United thing was still the great barrier across our progress. I was told in the city that we were doing well, but that we would never catch Manchester United.

Certainly it would have been easy to slip into that way of thinking. I recalled a night two seasons previously when we had gone to Leicester and won a Cup replay well. I went to sleep a contented man, confident that the morning papers would be full of fresh evidence that Manchester City were the rising force in the game, In fact, we got about three paragraphs in each paper. The story was, once again, Manchester United. They had won 5-1 at Benfica! George Best had played the game of his life. Thre was nothing to do but chip away. We had made certain progress, our crowds were beginning to swell, and at least United were now aware that there was another team in the city. That awareness came to a dramatic pitch the spring night we tossed them aside on our way to the First Division championship.

It was one of the great nights of my life. All my players rose to peaks of performance. Bell was staggering, a machine of awesome running power. Yet it started badly. United scored in the first minute and my plan for Book to mark Best tightly was in tatters. Best was over-running Book, a formidable feat. So I immediately told Book to play his normal game and wait for Best. It worked. Best lost some of his menace and Bell, Lee, and Summerbee began to stretch United at the seams. We were the much better conditioned team and our skill factor rose dramatically. We set up the championship win that night.

There was so much happiness among the City fans that evening. Years of humiliation had been, if not wiped away, at least eased. The balance of power was beginning to swing strongly in our direction. If you are not too tightly involved in football you may discount the feelings of the down-trodden supporters. In fact their team becomes an expression of themselves; their moods, their hopes, are tightly interwoven into the fate of the team. And that night at Old Trafford the supporters of Manchester City walked out of the wilderness.

Afterwards, Sir Matt Busby was as urbane as ever. But I sensed that we were beginning to get through to him. He is a man who hates to be second anywhere, and for it to happen to him in Manchester was quite a new experience.

The victory over United gave us the nerve and the momentum to stretch out for the title. But it was a hard, close run along the rails. We entered the final phase with a mid-week night match against Everton I sensed that the tension of the championship was beginning to get to us and if we were to stay in the battle we needed both points from the game at Maine Road.

Tony Book broke that tension when he raced into the penalty area and snaffled a goal from the toes of Everton. Almost as he scored the news came through that Manchester United were losing at West Bromwich. The atmosphere at Maine Road was electric. It meant that if we won our last two games, at Tottenham and Newcastle, we would be champions. In three years we would have travelled from nowhere to the peak of English football. It was a dramatic prospect.

The victory at Tottenham was a brilliant tactical success. We had the men to hit Spurs at their weakest point, the slowing Dave Mackay, and all our planning was geared to that. Francis Lee was required to draw Cyril Knowles out to the right touchline; the Spurs man had to counter those mazy, incredibly powerful little runs which I am delighted to see Lee still performing for Derby County and, ironically, Dave Mackay. And Summerbee, possibly the most pugnacious forward in the football league, would strike out to the left, pulling Mike England with him. The running and pressure of Lee and Summerbee was designed to set up our big play...to give Colin Bell a clear run at the vulnerable Mackay.

It worked beautifully. Summerbee and Lee at times had Knowles and England stretched 40 yards apart. Bell simply overwhelmed Mackay and we won 3-1. Bell was freakish, and he was slowly grasping what sort of talent he had inside him.

We laid siege to Newcastle. About 20,000 of our fans made the journey. Before the game Joe Harvey, the Newcastle United manager, said to me: "This is the first time I have been beaten at home before the game has started." We had put on a tremendous show of confidence. We knew that a point was of no use. I was happy about Lee, Summerbee and Bell. They were still full of their triumphs at Tottenham. But no one could have anticipated that the defence would have played so badly, so nervously. George Heslop for a time froze completely. He panicked every time the ball came near to him and this was alarming. Fortunately, the forwards were performing brilliantly again and we were two up in 20 minutes. Our defence, though, was determined to make a game of it. They let in two goals. But we had established an attacking rhythm andwent back to a 4-2 lead, with Francis Lee getting a superb goal disallowed. Newcastle did score again, but it was irrelevant, we were home.

I felt drained in the dressing room afterwards. People like Lee and Summerbee were jumping in and out of the bath, champagne corks were exploding, I couldn't quite catch the mood. The title had come to us on a flood tide. I think deep down I was a little bit stunned.

It was only later at a huge party in the Cabaret Club in Manchester that the scale of the achievement began to dawn on me. We had carried off the League title playing football which brimmed with skill and aggression. We had done more than win the championship. We had done it with football quite out of the pattern which had been laid down by England's World Cup success. We had proven that you could still win something big with five brilliant forwards. Lee, Summerbee, Bell, Young and Coleman had exploded as though out of a more colourful past.

Despite the fact that I had snatched just an hour's sleep at a girl friend's flat I was in an extravagant mood at the Maine Road press conference the following morning. I announced to the pressmen: "There's no limit on what this team can achieve. We will win the European Cup. We will terrorise Europe."

I felt acutely that we had come up with some original football. We had thrashed Manchester United, we had become a power in the land.

Only one thing could have spoiled that morning of triumph for me. That would have been the knowledge that within a month Manchester United, the red cloud over Maine Road, would be crowned European champions at Wembley. And even when it happened I was able to point out that no longer did the red shirts monopolise the city parks. Now it was running a mere 60–40 in their favour.

# Chapter Twelve

## The disenchanted

Something very chilling happened to me on a warm, clammy night in Istanbul in the autumn of 1968. Manchester City fell at the first hurdle of the European Cup. We lost to Fenerbache, a team so ill-considered that, unwisely, I hadn't even bothered to have them watched. I couldn't quite believe what was happening to my team in the concrete stadium overlooking the Golden Horn. The place was filled with hysterical Turks. It was like watching a slow-motion horror film. Before my eyes my players were simply freezing. Goalkeeper Ken Mulhearn was rooted in panic, letting in two terrible goals. George Heslop seemed unable to move coherently. Even the swaggering 'baby-face', Tony Coleman, found himself unable to play.

We lost 2-1, having been only able to draw at Maine Road. It was a colossal flop. I had been so sure we would cut a fiery path through European football. At that championship press conference in the spring I had announced that European football was filled with cowards, people who would simply turn and run against the force and aggression which had become the style of Manchester City. And as the newspaper men happily revived those earlier headlines, I sat bleakly fending off questions in a hotel lounge. Maybe I had been a bit cocky about this first tie. I should have watched the Turks beforehand, if only to guard against complacency from the team. But the defeat had come because our team had simply not played. I remember groaning in the dug-out: "They look like Girl Guides."

One basic misconception had undone me. It is one that is being slowly discarded by all but a few die-hards in English football. I mean the theory that the Football League is the toughest competition in the world. In terms of physical effort it may still be true. But in the matter of skill and class we have slipped behind. I thought that because we had won the First Division championship we were suddenly a great side. I was badly wrong. In Turkey it came home to me that I still had some very ordinary players. Just as with England when the World Cup was carried off in 1966.

My belief that we would terrorise Europe had come from watching a lot of Continental football, and from listening to the defensive, cautious thoughts of Helenio Herrera and the Benfica chief Bella Guttman. And at Old Trafford I had sat beside Rinus Michels, creator of Ajax, watching AC Milan meet Manchester United. He amazed me when he said: "I hope United win because I think Milan would be too strong for us." I was staggered that a man with Cruyff and Kaizer in his team could be afraid of anyone. I thought I had detected fear when in fact there may have been an undertone of realism.

Certainly Turkey brought me and the team back to earth. We had a summer of complete high spirits. There had been a tour of the United States, a great, colourful sweep through New York, Atlanta, San Francisco, Los Angeles, Mexico City and then Atlanta again. We had witnessed a gun battle in our hotel; Coleman and Stan Bowles had been arrested by cops who impressed their seriousness by firing shots into the pavement, and in Atlanta the lady proprietor of a local radio station had tried to persuade me to abandon football and stay with her. We were virtually chased out of Mexico City when it was learned that we play our second team goalkeeper at centre forward, that we had just nine players available, and that our internationals were away with England.

In San Francisco I went with Francis Lee to a place called the Red Garter. It is a terribly patriotic place where the patrons spend the evening drinking cold beer, eating peanuts placed in great bowls on the tables, and singing the glories of Uncle Sam. Francis Lee was non-plussed. He started eating the flowers from a table vase. Then he asked the people on the next table if they wanted their flowers. It was a somewhat extravagant tour. I recall Neil Young and George Heslop returning to the hotel whitefaced. They had left a cinema and called into a bar for a hamburger. A row had developed and two people were shot.

We made a poor start to the new season and the Turkish result came like a firm slap in the face. Perhaps we needed it.

Certainly once we got into our FA Cup run I couldn't see any team stopping us. We were drawn at Newcastle and outplayed then before 55,000 fans. The game ended in a goalless draw, but we rolled over them at Maine Road. We got Everton in the semi-final at Villa Park and on the face of it it looked a very tough game. Everton had developed very smoothly that season and most people fancied them.

Before the game I gave probably my best-ever team talk. We were going to close them up, absorb some punishment, and then strike at them. Even though Mike Doyle was off the field for seventeen minutes we were never in danger. Tommy Booth, the boy who had taken over from Heslop at centre half, got up to score our winning goal. We had 'psyched' Everton out of the Cup and we took the same aggressive attitude into the final, when we beat Leicester City 1-0.

Before the next Christmas we had ensured another Wembley place, in the final of the League Cup. Manchester

United had fallen to us in the two-legged semi-finals. We were also a different proposition in the European Cup-winners Cup, blasting through to the final against Gornik.

We won both finals and the first of them, the League Cup in March, was carried against the odds. We had to play a European tie in Portugal in the mid-week before the final with West Bromwich Albion and we had injury problems. We also had difficulty with fog-bound airports and we reached London in an exhausted condition. But out of the crisis there came a formation which worked beautifully. We packed the defence, and had Glyn Pardoe breaking out of midfield. Francis Lee played probably the best game of his life. He didn't score but his relentless running gradually wore down an Albion side who had the encouragement of an early goal by Jeff Astle. We needed extra time but there was no question about us winning. Pardoe got up for the deciding goal.

In Vienna for the final of the Cup-winners Cup we tried desperately to get Mike Summerbee fit. He had a leg injury. We gave him injections, we considered gambling on his courage and his fierce instinct for competition. But we had to leave him out. The first minutes of the game soothed my fears. Neil Young scored an early goal and later Francis Lee scored a penalty. The Poles of Gornik, who had been surprised by the force of our early play, got a goal back but they never really threatened us. There was a great reception at Vienna City Hall, and a night of celebration. Once again we had come through to take the big prizes. It had become a pattern of success. We had grown into true winners.

Dawn broke gloriously over the city. I had had perhaps two hours sleep, but I felt well when I went out on to the hotel balcony. Vienna, a city I had known as an ambitious, hopeful young man, was in blossom and as I looked out from that balcony I could not have imagined that it would be, at the very least, five years before I tasted again the special flavour of winning something big.

I didn't know that there would be some terrible, breathtaking disappointments to follow; that the euphoria of Vienna was in fact a climax to the rampaging years which carried Manchester City out of the shadow of Manchester United and into the forefront of English and European football. I saw Vienna as merely a milestone on a road to be littered with broken opponents.

And, looking back, I do not believe that was unreasonable. Harry Godwin, the chief scout, had worked hard and well and some exciting young players were emerging at the club. Willie Donachie, a Scottish International, Tony Towers, now with Sunderland and included in the plans of England manager Don Revie, and Derek Jeffries, from whom I still expect much at Crystal Palace, were beginning to challenge for places in the team. It is also true that the team had become conditioned to success. They had formed a taste and a need to win.

Any review of those post-Vienna days must include criticism of myself. I have already explained the mood of impatience and frustration which was growing within me. I could begin to grasp that Joe Mercer was reluctant to give me my head. And feelings began to be bottled up. Some of that free spirit which had been such a crucial factor in the club's success was dwindling. Francis Lee, possibly the best footballer character who has ever played for me, came to me one day and said: "Mal, you will have to get rid of two players. They're mixing it in the dressing room. If you don't stop it now it could spread." I don't give their names because they are still in football and everybody deserves a second chance, but I sold them almost immediately.

Season 70-71 was a grim anti-climax. It was the first time since 1967—our year of consolidation in the First Division—that we finished empty-handed. We did reach the semi-finals of the Cup-winners Cup. That might have persuaded some clubs that they had had a reasonable year. But for us it was the dregs at the bottom of a bottle of wine.

My relations with Joe Mercer had deteriorated. The Boardroom was aflame with the take-over bid that I, in a mood of desperation, had inspired. Summer came as a relief.

I took control the following winter and as we pushed into 1972, with Francis Lee having his best season, goals flowing from him in an apparently endless stream of aggression, I sensed that we would strike gold again. Towers, in midfield, was developing marvellously. We edged to the top of the First Division.

It was then that I made my big move—one that some people in the game described as my one major error in the transfer market. I signed Rodney Marsh. They said it was madness to import a highly individual player into a side striking out for the First Division championship. Why not let well alone?

It is thinking which has never had any appeal for me. Marsh was available. I considered him the most spectacular English player next to George Best—and George was then entering into his decline. By now I had collected that £10 bet with Paddy Crerand about Manchester City not being able to get more than 30,000 fans into Maine Road, but it was still true that our gates were painfully low compared with Old Trafford. In every respect we had a better, more skilful side yet the old mists of legend still enveloped United. They were still the team who drew the big crowd. I believed that Rodney's touch of theatre, his marvellous skill, could be the element which finally snapped United's hold in the city.

Rodney was overweight and out of condition when I arrived back with him at Manchester's Ringway Airport. I wasn't too happy with the way his leather coat tugged at his thighs. But the papers exploded with exactly the sort of publicity I had hoped for. Marsh, the clown prince of City; the headlines screamed about our glamorous new signing. I kept him on ice for 10 days. He came to watch us in our Saturday match at Everton. We won 1-0 in a swirling wind. The pressure was building on the boy—and also on myself.

His first game was against Chelsea at Maine Road. The crowd was well above average. Rodney arrived at the ground at 10 in the morning, pale and drawn. He hadn't slept. We won 1-0, but the game was a disaster for Rodney. He showed, of course, that he was a player of thrilling skill. But his lack of fitness showed too clearly. I withdrew him 10 minutes before the end. He was shattered, possibly as much by nervous tension as physical exhaustion.

Rodney took time to settle, and we lost a game to Stoke.

Our title pursuit was in crisis when we went down to Southampton. Again, Rodney couldn't really get into the game. Bell played poorly, and Francis Lee, after doing so much to get us into the challenging position, was running out of steam—at an alarming rate. Francis in fact had personal problems. His business affairs went through a crisis and at the end of the season he collapsed and had to go into hospital. We lost at Southampton. The Marsh thing was exploding in my face.

We came back with a home victory over West Ham United, and Rodney scored two goals. But I wasn't swayed by that. I felt he still needed time to get properly fit. I caused a sensation on the eve of our League match with Manchester United. I dropped Rodney Marsh—just weeks after paying a club record fee of £200,000. It was a decision that needed as much nerve as the one to go out and buy him. But in both cases I felt I was right. We played shakily at first, conceded an early goal, but gradually we pushed United back and Lee, finding again briefly his earlier momentum, scored two goals. We went into the last quarter 2-1 ahead. Doyle had got a bit of an injury and I replaced him with Marsh. He played perhaps the most dazzling 20 minutes of his career, demoralising Scottish international Martin Buchan with a series of outrageous runs down the flanks, and then scored a sweetly volleyed goal.

We missed the title by a point. Ipswich Town, playing with an incredible fierceness in view of the fact that they were out of the reckoning, beat us 2-1 in the last but one game. That killed us. The inquests in Manchester were particularly hard on me, and they centred on the signing of Marsh. Did I make a mistake? I suppose it depends on how wide a view you are prepared to take of the situation at Maine Road, then. I felt that I was doing something for the club which in fact went beyond the winning of a title, however important that goal was.

In Manchester we had extraordinary competition. Our rivals were not merely another football team, they were something woven into the life of the city, and if Colin Bell, Francis Lee and Mike Summerbee were all exceptionally gifted players they did lack that quality of fantasy which Marsh brought to his game. Nor do I believe that anything is as simple as the statement that we lost the title because of Rodney Marsh's arrival. It's also true that Francis Lee—a giant all seasons—suddenly dwindled. And Colin Bell had some appalling games.

There was, too, a savage irony about our last League game of the season. We played Derby County, who heard that they had won the title, almost by default, in their Majorca hotel when Liverpool failed to win at Arsenal. We slaughtered Derby County and Rodney's performance was astonishing. He toyed with people like Roy McFarland, scored a tremendous goal after an incredible run to the edge of the box and won the penalty which made the game safe for us. It was, out of defeat, an extraordinary statement of his skill...and a promise of what he would bring to the club in the future. I felt a sad sort of vindication that afternoon.

I also suspect that if you asked Manchester City fans today whether I did the right thing in signing Marsh they would answer a firm yes. They have learned to live with his extravagances, his inconsistencies. It is, after all, the inevitable price you pay for the promise of magic.

So I failed by a point to carry off the championship in my

first year of full control. That was a measure of my failure. I was shattered, of course. But I did not shelter behind the narrowness of that failure. I knew we should have won the title, that we had the players to do it.

And the new season brought some disastrous results. We lost our first two games to the Merseyside clubs—and we didn't play. I was very worried but not to the extent of some people who thought the team was breaking up. We had too much quality at the club for that. I did believe that the pre-season preparation had included too many friendly games. It took us some time to get off the bottom of the table, but we did begin to get this feeling about an FA Cup run—even when we were drawn away to Liverpool in the fourth round. I 'psyched' out Liverpool. At that time I was writing a column for the Daily Express and the northern editions devoted most of their back page to a piece in which I claimed: "We will bury the myth of Liverpool." I argued that Liverpool hadn't won anything, that their reputation was inflated, and that we would expose all their limitations. Bill Shankly was furious. He called me a madman. But I think he may also have recognised an element of truth in what I said. That was a piece of the old psychological warfare, but I did know that my team was in tremendous shape for the game. Our play had come together nicely after the early season problems. We were ready to take on Liverpool before the Kop.

We drew 0-0 and Liverpool claimed that we had roughed them up. The press took up that claim—but I considered it nonsense. We had simply matched Liverpool in every phase of the game and the roughness came in the fierceness of the competition in the middle of the pitch. Liverpool were not used to being held on their ground, and they were a bit rattled. It just wasn't a contest at Maine Road. Emlyn Hughes made a few hopeful gallops but we picked them off, winning 2-0. I couldn't see how anyone could stop us in the Cup after that performance. We drew Sunderland at home in the next round. For the first half of the game they scarcely touched the ball. Their manager, Bob Stokoe, said later, "I thought that I would have to throw another ball on the pitch for us to get a kick." Tony Towers scored an early goal and it was all a bit effortless. Until Joe Corrigan sent the ball to the feet of the Sunderland player Mickey Horswill. He couldn't believe his good luck as he shot Sunderland back into the Cup and, eventually, their historic defeat of Leeds at Wembley. We took the tie to a replay at Sunderland, but our moment had gone.

That, I suppose, brought the curtain down on me at Maine Road. I was under no pressure for my job. In fact I could have done what so many people in football do. Sat on my backside and lived off the transfer market. But I had become disenchanted with the club. The directors had dragged their feet in giving me the sort of contract I wanted, and had been promised. The urgency and thrill had gone out of my work.

It was a desperately unhappy situation to be in after all the great times, the moments when Mercer, the players, and I had between us achieved a sort of working perfection.

When the Crystal Palace job became available in the March of 1973 I didn't feel a flicker of interest. When you have players like Bell, Lee, Summerbee, Marsh, Towers and Donachie at your disposal it is difficult to covet any other job in the game. But Palace chairman, Ray Bloye, asked if he could speak with me. I agreed to see him in London but I did point out that I wasn't interested in his job.

Bloye won me over very quickly. I liked his approach, which seemed to me bigger than almost any other football director I had spoken with. I couldn't imagine him putting the sort of petty, day-to-day restrictions on his manager that I had been suffering. He seemed as though he was looking for a man to do a job and would, having found him, say: "Right, you get on with it." I agreed to join Crystal Palace at the end of our interview.

Manchester City directors drove into Maine Road the morning I announced my decision. They tried to persuade me to say, offering me money to buy players, suggesting that we should have another look at my contract. They were offering too much, too late. But they couldn't budge me. Apart from the days in Italy when I lingered over the Juventus offer, I have always been a man of quick decision. I drove away from Maine Road without glancing back.

# Chapter Thirteen

## On the wild side

At the Café Royal in London on a warm, May night in 1969, a big, very bald man sat at a banqueting table with large tears rolling down his cheeks. He was my great, villainous friend Joe Lowery. He was sitting among other old friends of mine at Manchester City's celebration banquet following the Cup Final. The tears, he told me, were the natural reaction of a man attending his first great sporting occasion after five years in prison.

I don't know where Joe got the surname Lowery from. He came out of the East End with one of those Jewish names which are too much—far stronger than, say, Finkelstein. He was a villain, an extremely tricky character, but he was also my friend. I had him at the banquet because behind the villainy and the trickery, the trouble and embarrassment he had caused me—once the police hauled me off for hours of questioning after I had been seen talking with him at Doncaster racecourse—there was a great generosity of spirit. In many ways Joe Lowery represented that part of my life I most wanted to forget, the times when I brushed perilously close to a life of crime. But if I could reject the associations I could not reject the man.

He had a big, fat, lovely face and he was always

immaculately dressed. I always think of him when I see the television cop Kojak.

I first met him at Hackney dog track. John Dick, Vic Keeble, Noel Cantwell, and I used to go along there hopefully each week. We were all on about £15 a week, and almost invariably one of us would have to go back to the club offices for a £5 sub. Joe approached me one afternoon with a concerned expression on his face. He said: "What are you doing, son? You're losing your money again. You boys don't have a chance here. Listen, I want you and your friends to do some work for me. Here's £80, put some money on for me." We laid on the forecast bets for Joe. Then he gave me the key to his car, a big Ford, saying: "Get me £500 from the spare tyre in the boot." There must have been £5- to £6,000 in tight bundles rolled into the tyre. We put £300 to win on one dog, and then £200 on a forecast. When we gave Joe the winning tickets he handed me £80 to share among the lads. We couldn't really believe we were getting so much money for such simple work.

If I'm honest I must admit that I suspected Joe was into some sort of racket. But he protected us. He never implicated us. He simply asked us to put money on dogs. We were his runners.

I suppose I got my first clear inkling that Joe was doping dogs at the Clapton track.

It seemed strange that Joe was asking us to lay so much money on a certain dog when the race had one clear favourite, a very fast animal owned by Sir Alf Ramsey, then known more simply as Alf, the Dagenham 'darkie' and right back for Spurs. It was a hurdle race and Alf's dog hurtled towards the first obstacle—then collapsed a couple of yards short. I was standing next to Joe as the track exploded with angry yells. It looked very bad, and Joe murmured to himself: "Sod me, I gave it too much. It should have gone with the hurdle."

Joe Lowery took a lower profile after that incident. But I

think he knew that he was slowly being identified as the man at the head of a doping operation and very soon he was warned off the dog tracks. He then moved in the world of racing. When the favourite failed badly in the St. Leger at Doncaster he was at last getting into real trouble. Apparently the police had been dogging him for weeks and when they saw me in deep conversation with him they assumed I was also involved. In fact we had been talking about the old times on the dog tracks. I wasn't involved in any coup, but the police took a lot of persuading. They gave me a four-hour grilling, broken only by the arrival of Arthur Shaw. With his help I was able to get out of the place.

But the police had assembled a strong case against Joe. Soon he was serving the first of two five-year stretches in an open prison in the West Country. I wrote to him, sent him some gear for the prison football team. When he came out I did what I could to help him.

A few days before the 1969 Cup Final—and our winning banquet—I had a call from him, asking me to see him in the Beachcomber bar at the Mayfair Hotel. Even when things were at their worst Joe preserved some style. We had a few drinks and he told me that he needed £200 very desperately. I could sense that he hated asking me. But I gave it to him without thinking. I found the appeal of this man irresistible. He was the sort of man who would make thousands on crooked horse racing coups—and then gamble the money straight. He was also very generous. I know that in one betting coup the return was £30,000. Joe and two partners shared £9,000 and a co-operative stable lad got £3,000. Six weeks after that I recall Joe coming up to me saying: "Malcolm, lend me a tenner, I've got to fill the car with petrol." He was very concerned about coming to the banquet. He thought somebody might recognise him and that it would reflect badly on me. But I insisted. Joe came from a murky corner of my past, but I wasn't about to disown him for that. He stepped over the mark many times

142

in his life and he paid his price.

He died within a year of that banquet. Prison, I suppose, had broken him. You may feel that I have attempted to glorify a crook, a man whose business in life was to cheat millions of punters out of a legitimate wager and it is a point I do recognise. But then I am not a man to throw stones. There are things about my own life which I regret deeply.

Once I got on the fringe of a pornography racket. An American came into my club one day with a proposition. He had got hold of a list of people—very rich people—living in and around London, who formed a ready and lucrative market for porn. My job would be simple. I would collect the letters and money from a box number address. There was a lot of cash involved and this was very tempting. My financial position was as rocky as ever. But it was something I found I couldn't live with. Debts had become a constant factor in my life, but to get deeply involved in something like this was an entirely different matter.

I decided to continue the running battle with my bank manager. That such temptations should come in my path was not surprising. I had grown up with villains.

I knew friends of the Great Train Robber Buster Edwards and there was a feeler for me to give evidence on his behalf at the Old Bailey.

These are aspects of life which can ensnare you if you mix with a wide circle of people, if you spend your money rashly, and you have a tendency to treat people as you find them. Joe Lowery was the classic case. Had I been a steadier type, I suppose, a hundred warning bells would have rung when he made his first approach to me at Hackney Dog Track. But his manner was friendly, he supported West Ham United, and there was a twinkle of humour about him. He was also the sort of man who, having made a friend, would never let him down. Almost all the players at West Ham had reason to be grateful for him. His tips augmented our poor wages. I learned years later that even the young apprentices at Upton Park used to act on the information which filtered down to them through the club. Yet, I have to admit, he was a criminal, a man whose whole upbringing was geared to making money unlawfully.

My own instinct has always been to gamble. I'm hopeless with money because I have never quite been able to assess its worth.

When I have it I spend it—and also, I have to admit, I sometimes spend it when it isn't there.

At the end of my racing days with Arthur Shaw, when I had already decided that ultimately you couldn't beat the bookmakers, I had one last, wild effort. And lost £1,500. It was money I just couldn't pay. The bookmakers pressed hard and when I failed to come up with the money I was warned off the tracks. It was not a pleasant sensation and it more or less broke the hard edge of my gambling instinct. Eventually the ban was lifted and when—years later—I found myself banned from football for a month I did go on another spree, at Sandown Park. That business exploded in my face after my move to Crystal Palace in 1973. Someone at William Hills leaked it to the press that I owed them more than £1,000. The club Chairman wiped that away with one sweep of his pen. But it was another sharp jolt; a sort of public reminder to me that a reckless streak could still lead to much self-damage. Even on the eve of my wedding I had been unable to restrain the urge to speculate. It was before Joe Lowery had started to guide me towards the bookmaker's stall, and I lost £80. It meant I approached my wedding day with two shillings in my pocket. Fortunately, my friend Derek Ufton owed me £26 and I was able to claim that rather forcefully. But it didn't run to a honeymoon.

The absurd thing is that money is not important to me. Once Arthur Shaw and I took a heavy beating at the races. It was a bit of a disaster for me. I was really struggling. But after I had dropped Arthur off in Twickenham Green, then driven across London, I got into a tracksuit and ran through the streets around my home. With each stride the pressures seemed to lift.

I suppose some of my financial scrapes would have driven many men to distraction. Twice finance companies have re-claimed cars. And for months in Manchester I used to go into Maine Road by bus. My bank manager there was a hard-pressed but tolerant man—and sometimes he showed a flash of humour. Once he wrote to me asking for some match tickets, adding the P.S. "I shall be writing to you in my usual tone very soon." I suppose Manchester saw me in particularly hectic form. With Fred Pye a well-known character in the City and in football, who had made a lot of money out of scrap metal—and a businessman Jimmy Walsh I was involved in opening a restaurant called Napoleons. It was a lavish enterprise. But I'm afraid it was doomed.

I think I was the most regular customer—and that was the big problem. One morning, soon after the place had opened, the manager rang Freddie Pye to report a very good night's business. "We took £300." He then added that I had been in with a big party, run up a bill for £98, signed the cheque and said I would pay later. I gather that Fred gave a little groan. The business folded two years later with losses of about £20,000. I suppose I had given it an extravagant kiss of death.

Once I recall going on holiday with Noel Cantwell to Majorca. When we had settled the wives in their plane seats I had to confess to Noel that I had sixpence in my pocket. I wrote a cheque which I suspected might bounce. It did.

I also wrote a cheque for £27,000 one night in Copenhagen—then rang my bank the following day to cancel it. The incident was not quite as sinister as it sounds. John Charles and I went into a nightclub after a match in the city, and we had a good party going. The owner was particularly impressed to have a footballing celebrity like Charles in the place.

But there was a snag. He wanted to close up the place at 3 a.m. We had been talking about John Charles's business interests in Italy and it occurred to me that this particular club would be a nice addition to his foreign investments. And if he should buy it on the spot he would then be the man to decide when the place should close. I wrote the cheque. And the drinks flowed until dawn broke over the city.

I do not recall the wildness, the great extravagances with pride. It may be that some people would regard my private life as a disaster area. All I can say is that I have tried to live it to the full. And if I have taken much out of it, I have also put into it all that I have. In the case of Joe Lowery it was a couple of hundred pounds and a place at a Cup final banquet.

# Chapter Fourteen

## The sweet taste of failure

If you ever want to see all the faces of football, the ones puffed up with success, the others, more numerous, haggard with failure, you should go along to the annual dinner of the Football Writers' Association. They are all there. Even Sir Alf Ramsey attends, though these days he has the air of a C.O. spending some time in the sergeants' mess. Once he said to me: "Tell me, Malcolm, is Francis Lee a spiv?" I replied: "Do you mean like your brothers, Alf?" There are good, decent men like Dave Sexton, who had known great success and also the bitterness of being sacked. He once was so intense he threw a packet of chewing gum at me during a game in which his player Ron Boyle was sent off. They all gather, the good and the bad, the brave and the terrified, just two days before the Cup Final. But for the two competing clubs it is the end of another battle to stay alive in the game and perhaps, if you have had the breaks or you have done your work well enough, there is some success. People look at each other and set categories, like winners, losers, and people who might have chances or are almost certainly dead.

In the May of 1974 I went along for the first time as a failure. I didn't think of myself as a failure. But I knew that was how it must have looked to a lot of the people crammed into the banqueting hall of the Bloomsbury Centre. Some people said things like "Bad luck, Mal" but their eyes told a different story.

My club Crystal Palace had gone straight down through the Second Division. In the January I had offered my resignation to the Chairman Ray Bloye, a man who had shown great faith in me and had behaved so well and with such understanding that I felt all the disappointments doubly. It had been a new and appalling experience to find myself being crushed by results, week after week they came like a succession of hammer blows. At Cambridge University, Bath, Toronto, Plymouth, and most of all at Manchester the tide had flowed strongly with me.

It is true that Plymouth Argyle did sack me. But the day they did that to me I had gone to the ground dressed in my best suit, smoking a big cigar, and I laughed at them. I knew I was being dismissed for my independence, my indiscretions, and my life style. They couldn't touch me on football. But the business at Crystal Palace had been something else. I knew I couldn't do anything with the team I inherited from Bert Head. Palace had been kept in the First Division, certainly, but the structure of the club was so diseased that the moment I began to touch it, it crumbled in my fingers. Since I left Manchester City in 1973 they have had three managers, Johnny Hart, who cracked under the pressure, Ron Saunders, who was sacked, and my man Tony Book, taking his first stride in management. And never has there been a question of their being neglected. Because the structure was strong and healthy.

At Palace I tried to graft on new and better players, boys like Peter Taylor and Derek Jeffries, and then found that there was no way that I could merely tinker with the team. I had to demolish and then build again, on a decline. I said that Christmas would mark the point where we began to look like a team. And in the last half of the season there were remarkable results. Arsenal, Queen's Park Rangers, and Chelsea all offered huge fees for Peter Taylor and as Easter approached we looked certain to avoid the drop. But tensions returned and we faltered over the holiday games. We outclassed Fulham at Craven Cottage on Good Friday, then threw all the advantage away at Millwall—and on the following Tuesday, Bobby Moore, of all people played immaculately at our ground and Fulham beat us soundly. We could only draw our last match at Cardiff, where a win would have guaranteed us safety.

But I did go to the Bloomsbury Centre feeling that some things had been rescued from the disaster. The club had got rid of a lot of indifference, the wage bill was more realistic, and the training routine was no longer something out of the dark ages. There was no way that I could feel triumphant. I had lost too many hours sleep for that. I had paced the floor of my Kensington flat endlessly in the small hours, perhaps making myself a cup of tea at 5 in the morning. Yet for all the blows and the horrors—in one night match, Palace, winning 1-0, lost the game in the last two minutes—I didn't really taste the flavour of being among the losers until I moved through the crush of the Bloomsbury Centre.

I tasted it so strongly, as the speeches droned on, that it took some of my friends to restrain me from getting up on the top table and making an unscheduled speech. They argued that it would almost certainly be misinterpreted. I had had a couple of drinks and they wanted to protect me from sneers.

That speech is still unmade. But the sense and feeling of it has remained inside me. It is a gut thing. I would have talked that night about the margins which separate the winners and the losers, of the vague dividing line which isn't always marked by ability. I knew now what it was to be on both sides of the line and I felt I had some things to say which were worth saying. I wanted to become the spokesman for the losers on this night which celebrates, above all, the men who have emerged from the brilliant

149

lottery of the FA Cup. There would have been some harsh things to say. I would have said that there were a lot of compromisers and cowards in football and that often the system, which beneath a thin veneer of respectability is incredibly cynical and sometimes corrupt, most favoured those who were ready to be two-faced and even dishonest. I would have made it clear that I didn't have too much respect for the criteria of success and failure in the game, or the majority of the men who occupied positions of most power. I would have said that the authority in the game was too often a sick joke. And I suppose people would have said; "What right has he got to talk? He's taken Crystal Palace to the Third Division."

I suppose those things were better left unsaid then. Instead I spent an hour or so talking with Joe Mercer about his forthcoming summer tour as manager of the England team for home internationals and games in Europe.

My speech might have seemed like a cry from the gallows, the self-justification of a condemned man. In fact it would have been something more than that. I have never seen football as an area where the end justifies the means. A series of defeats at Crystal Palace had brought certain basic truths into focus.

Running through my mind also would have been the experiences of Ian Greaves. I doubt if any single individual in the game had impressed me more than this man in recent years. His experiences have been even more devastating than mine. He guided Huddersfield Town out of the Second Division. He gave the club a face-lift. He was clearly a worker, a man who was giving everything he had to his club. And I watched him closely as Huddersfield found themselves unable to maintain their First Division position. I saw him live with the pressures of being relegated from First to Second, and then Third...and then the ultimate pressure of being sacked. I watched him and I was very impressed.

His best moment was probably the one that determined

150

his fate. I mean the time when he refused to bow to the demands of three of his players, Frank Worthington, Trevor Cherry and Roy Ellom. The club were in a critical position when they came to him—it was a crucial phase of the effort to avoid relegation from the First Division—and he believed that they had given him an ultimatum which meant: "Promise us better terms and we will pull the club out of trouble." He showed them the door and immediately transfer listed them.

How many people in football go through their careers without producing a piece of moral courage to compare with that. Greaves's decision meant his team was broken as a First Division force. But in that club he had preserved integrity. He had made it clear that he was a man who wouldn't put a convenient solution to a crisis in front of his principles. When I read of his decision I held up my hands in admiration. And the next time I saw him I said: "Whatever happens to you son, I give you 10 out of 10." Huddersfield Town sacked Ian Greaves when they reached the Third Division.

Such developments make you think seriously about the definition of success and failure. Brian Clough and Peter Taylor revitalised Derby County to an incredible extent. Yet now Peter Taylor struggles at Brighton and Clough seeks to re-establish his reputation at Nottingham Forest. For me, Clough did more in his five years at Derby than any of say 10 First Division managers in all their careers. There are many big-name managers who would be defeated by the problems of running a small club.

Ian Greaves has now returned to management with Bolton Wanderers. I know that he will do his work honestly and that he is one of those rare men in the game who do not compromise themselves. I remember early last season—my first as a Third Division manager—losing badly at Halifax. It is a ramshackle little ground and I felt terribly depressed. George Mulhall, Halifax's manager, was scarcely elated by victory. He knew that he was facing the sack. Mulhall took me into his pokey little office, along with Greaves. He produced a bottle of scotch. I don't drink scotch and I didn't feel like taking the glass he offered me. But Greaves said to me: "Malcolm, take a drink and don't let this game get you down. You know what you can do—you know what you have done." Greaves said that with great feeling. It was the result of a sharp education in the realities of football management.

So many managers live off the transfer market. They know that nothing pleases directors more than to sell a player, and make a quick, impressive looking profit. They might have a team that is becalmed in mediocrity but as long as financial pressure, and that of relegation, is off the directors, they know their jobs are safe. I had the opportunity to live in such a situation after the great years at Maine Road. But instead I took the challenge of Palace. It has been more difficult than I could have imagined, but sometimes the best things in your life come to you only through the extremes of difficulty. At Crystal Palace I know I have to be patient. This is not so hard when you can see that progress, real progress, is being made. I have the most individual coaching staff in the country and a scouting organisation which is beginning to embarrass the big London clubs.

I have at the back of my mind an achievement which will really knock some people sideways. It is an ambition which I think can only be formed by someone who has known very great successes, and then some terrible failure. You see I want people to acknowledge that I have gone into a tight situation, fought it, and then say "He's a man among boys ... he knows what he is doing and where he is going."

These experiences at Palace, in fact, have cleared away certain vague areas of my thinking about the game. I have become obsessed with teaching, with getting to the heart of reality. I have read more in the last two years than in the rest of my life. It is an urge to get through the gloss and the pretence, and to deal only with facts.

I know now what I have to do. It is very simple and very exciting.

# Chapter Fifteen

## Supercoach

Helenio Herrera is small, sallow-skinned, and very short-sighted; a long way, in fact, from the image of Supercoach. His dramatic effect, which is very biting and also subtle, comes when he assembles a group of players on a training pitch. There is absolute organisation and precision about his work. He becomes a Svengali with a whistle. I first watched him work at Lilleshall, the old manor house set in the Shrophire meadows which has been coverted into the FA's coaching centre. It was a fascinating sight. He spoke the universal language of football, though I noticed that he obscured exactly how well he could speak English. It was as though he was using that as an extra element of strength. Some press men turned up to watch one of his sessions and the result was startling. His whistle became a conductor's baton. He bamboozled the press with a spectacular routine which had more to do with theatre than football...but it explained to me some of the reason for his success. He brought things to life almost effortlessly. There was precision, but also a rich dash of imagination.

Herrera, it seemed to me, had caught the secret of relentlesss coaching without boredom. As I watched him work in the sunshine a lot of things came alive for me. And when, soon afterwards, I took charge of a class I was very conscious of Herrera gazing at me intently. It was a rather intimidating experience. But I was also stimulated. I knew I was performing before a great ringmaster.

I was still making my way in the game and although I had certain belief in my ability to transmit ideas to players, I couldn't get it out of my brain that I was being watched by the best-paid man in football. As coach of Inter Milan, Herrera was known throughout Italian football as the Black Magician. It was a title he rejoiced in. When he walked out into the great concrete bowl of the San Siro stadium the place erupted. He was the master of Italy's most powerful team...and both the players and the fans were his puppets. I strained to make a good impression—but evidently I did not overdo it. I gave clear instructions to the players and I did a bit of shouting to get the message through clearly. Later, in a dressing room, Herrera came up to me and said: "Mr. Allison, those things you were doing were very good. You can be a great coach."

That, I suppose, was like a young jazz musician getting the nod from Duke Ellington. Certainly it is hard to describe how much that praise meant to me. For years I had been beating my head against a brick wall. Perhaps I had been too strong, perhaps too impudent, in my disgust at the training methods of my clubs Charlton and West Ham. Once I had brought back some training schedules from Lilleshall—they had been typed out by a University man, Jim Clarkson—and they were adopted by West Ham. A television crew came along to Upton Park to film our work and the manager, Ted Fenton, called me into his office and said that I had to organise things for the television people. I felt he was floundering. We were a professional football club with a manager and a training staff and yet no one could step forward and do the job properly. It seemed a crazy situation. But to be acknowledged by a man of Herrera's quality and prestige justified all those desperate journeys up to Shropshire.

155

Those journeys were inspired by one very basic question: "How do you properly train a professional footballer?" That I did become a top coach, offered in my time a Herrera-style contract by the wealthiest club in Italy, flowed, I suppose naturally, from the feelings that had welled up in me almost from my first days as a professional footballer. I have already discussed the disillusionment I felt at the Valley and Upton Park. Out of that disenchantment came an obsession with the problem of communicating.

Some people talk about communication as though it is a very simple thing, a matter perhaps only of clear language, and they are the worst communicators because they take too much for granted. In fact communicating is the most difficult thing in the world—certainly in football. You can tell somebody something, he can nod his head, and you can assume, quite wrongly, that the message has been absorbed. But it is not like a schoolmaster writing something down on the blackboard and his student copying it. You have to get inside both the mind and the instincts of a footballer. You have to hammer information into his subconscious, set up instinctive patterns of thought and reaction. And you have to keep on doing it until the thought process is removed. You have to get things so that they flow naturally out of a player. And technique and skills are only one aspect. The central challenge is to motivate the languid, the over-confident, and the insecure. It has always been for me the most fascinating work and just recently, since I have taken the job of building around a very young team at Crystal Palace, the challenge of it all has redoubled.

The urge to teach, to coach, though, did not carry me to Lilleshall. It was a much more selfish impulse. I wanted to make myself a better player and when I saw details of a coaching course on Upton Park notice board I thought that this might be my last chance. I had abandoned hope of getting any meaningful help from within the club.

At Charlton I had done a little basic coaching with younger players like Eddie Firmani and Stuart Leary, simple techniques in kicking and heading the ball. Things like dropping your head when you kick the ball. The head is the heaviest part of the body, and when it is lowered everything else falls into its correct place. I got that from studying a picture of a great kicker of the ball. And when you go to head the ball you jump off one foot and not two. You get so much more thrust and direction that way. It was all very basic, pathetic really when you consider that this was supposed to be a professional business and that there were people about who were being paid to do a job that they had never understood. But there is a limit to self-education and when I tried to help other people often I was doing so out of ignorance. There were great gaps in my knowledge. And certainly when I first arrived at Lilleshall and met Walter Winterbottom I felt I was coming face to face with the messiah. Here was the man who would teach me how to teach. In fact for a long time it was rather confusing. Winterbottom was concentrating on very basic coaching formulas for use with schoolboys. I had sorted out such things for myself. I wanted something more advanced. I needed to push on.

I was encouraged by the fact that there were older, much more famous players seeking the same sort of insights. They included Stan Mortensen, Jimmy Hagan and Ronnie Suart. The only people of my age on the course were the Burnley pair, Jimmy Adamson and Jimmy McIlroy. And they had been sent by their manager Alan Brown. Though I quickly came to admire the gentle, clearly-spoken Winterbottom, he was not too much help to me at first. I think he felt I was wanting to run before I could walk and he pointed out that I was, after all, on a preliminary course. But I suppose it was enough to be in an atmosphere where people were talking intelligently about the game, where new ideas were being tried, and the old, tired training chores were being tossed contemptuously on one side. And the great breakthrough came when I was allowed to take a class of my own.

It was an ordeal, of course. But it was also perhaps the most thrilling challenge of my life. I knew I had certain natural assets. I could throw my voice a long way. I was big and I knew how to use my physique. Very quickly I realised that my future in football, whatever success I might grasp at as a player, lay ultimately in being a top coach.

It was true that the sum of my football knowledge was still slim, but I had learned to argue with people and effectively put across a case. For some time I had been the established dressing room lawyer at West Ham.

I had fought a series of battles with manager Fenton and chairman Reg Pratt. And it wasn't merely a question of rebellion for its own sake. I fought them only when I felt they had treated the players with a particular lack of respect.

Once I threatened to lead the team out on strike—15 minutes before the start of a League match with Nottingham Forest. Earlier in the week we had played a friendly match against an England Amateur team. A crowd of more than 20,000 had turned up. But the club refused to pay us a win bonus. When we got our pay slips I established that we were legally entitled to an extra £2 a head. It was the sort of cheap thing which was always driving me mad at West Ham. When Fenton came into the dressing room I said to him very calmly: "If we don't get that win bonus in the next five minutes we're not going to change for the game." I don't imagine many football managers have had that sort of ultimatum, but I don't regret my action. I would expect the same sort of treatment from players if I ever treated them so badly. Fenton came back with £22 in cash.

An earlier incident soured what had looked likely to be a promising relationship with chairman Pratt. I knew that I had made something of an impression on Pratt and the rest of the board with my enthusiasm for training and work with the youngsters at the club. But all that was wiped away when Cliff Lloyd, secretary of the young Players'

Union, started to fire the first shots in the battle to remove the disgusting maximum wage regulations.

Lloyd sent around a circular asking players to put down details of any 'under-the-counter' payments they might have received. It was part of his case that the maximum wage regulation was, as well as being the most glaring example of feudalism in the game, also being abused by the clubs. I was summoned to the presence of chairman Pratt. He said, in a rather arrogant way: "I don't imagine the players will be signing this union document." His tone and his manner were guaranteed to provoke me and I said to him: "We have all signed the document." It wasn't strictly true, but it would be as soon as I got out of his office. I enjoyed the spectacle of the blood draining from his face. He had been asked to argue on television that it was possible to run a football club without making some technically illegal payments.

It was in such confrontations with people like Pratt and Fenton that I gathered together the raw material of my progress at Lilleshall. I had learned to argue a case if I felt it was right. I had lost any reticence about disputing points. And at Lilleshall I could glean the knowledge of great football men. People like Alan Brown and George Smith, a predecessor of mine at Palace, impressed me enormously. They were men who had applied their brains to the game. I watched Herrera closely, of course. I was staggered by his attention to detail. I wasn't surprised to learn that he got some of his routines out of an army manual. In some sessions his whistle seemed to punctuate every movemnt. In others he would release the players into dazzling routines. He was a perfectionist ready to settle only for that moment when it becomes clear that the message has been absorbed. He had noted that the great teams play in combinations of four, so he worked in groups of six or seven players, exhausting all possibilities of making new connections between that number of players.

I also watched with great admiration the German Helmut

Schoen. He was a gentle, almost shy character. But you could see the sweep of his football vision. He put great emphasis on skill and movement, a philosophy which reached a fitting, if slightly fortunate, climax when his German team wn the 1974 World Cup final against the superb Dutch in Munich.

But if I felt admiration for the little, intense Herrera, and the big, smiling Schoen, I never felt awe. Neither struck me as having a great personality. I wondered about their ability to get inside the skin of their players. Certainly that was my ideal. At an early age I had seen all the great coaches of world football. And I reckoned I could compete. Those spells at Cambridge University, Bath, Toronto and Plymouth made me very sure about my ability to inspire footballers. I had got across to undergraduates, young semi-professionals, and some gnarled old pros. Now all I needed was to work with thoroughbred material. And two years into my job at Manchester City I had all the material I needed. Initially, the whole thrust of my interest in coaching had been one of self-interest. I had wanted to find out things which could help me stretch my own limited ability. But, of course, in the process I learned how to expand and develop players who might be much more naturally gifted. Such people as Francis Lee and Colin Bell. I got Rodney Marsh very late in his career, which is something I will always regret. I would have loved to have got Rodney at about the age of 15 or 16. He remains a great and fascinating player. But he could have been a sensation.

Francis Lee was in fact not so much of a challenge. All I had to do with him was encourage his aggression, remind him of all his natural assets, and perhaps point him to situations where he would be better able to exploit his power of shot and speed over short distances. We decided that his best terrain was along the left, a point which Sir Alf Ramsey never full grasped when Francis had his run with the England team.

Colin Bell did require more work, though not too much

on the technique of the game. I was more concerned with getting him to lift his own standards, of making him aware that he should be drawing more from his natural powers. This was someone whose skin I really wanted to get inside. He didn't seem to grasp his own freakish strength. He looked bewildered, saying that he thought his had been one of the better performances. I said to him, "You are a great header of the ball. You have a terrific shot—and you're the best, most powerful runner in the business. Every time you walk off the pitch unable to say that you were streets ahead of the other 21 players you have failed. It is as simple as that." It took a long time to hammer that point into Colin Bell. When he came to City he was a bit languid. He thought it was enough to be a good player and he wasn't always prepared to strike out for greatness. But I think the message has got through now.

He has now absorbed into his game that awareness that he should consistently make his superior qualities work on the pitch. And the transmission of such a point is the key to coaching. Certainly it became a crucial factor at Manchester City. For once it became apparent that Bell was reaching out for new levels of performance, a chain reaction occurred. Mike Doyle, not a hugely gifted player, became much more of a significant figure, and right through the team target levels were being raised. Such a pursuit of perfection is a thrilling sight. And it is the football coach's great justification.

Inevitably, a coach loses his edge with a certain set of players. In the last period at Manchester City I sensed that we had all become too familiar; a kind of complacency had taken hold of both myself and the players. It is at times that a man should either move on—or radically change the emphasis of his work.

With the help of Dr. John Brooks of Salford University I had learned much about the human body, its ability to perform under stress and its capacity for recovery after a maxium effort. And with the psychologist John Kane I had pushed into the role of psychology in sport, an area which is neglected to an incredible extent in this country. Both aspects fascinate me, and now that I believe the scuffling, battling period at Crystal Palace is being replaced by a time when we can begin to measure our strides, I intend to spend more of my time adapting the latest thought in both fields. It is work which for me has no boundaries other than the ones man creates for himself.

I also have a new and stronger conception of the way to truly coach and develop a football team. It is the result of much study, experience, and the lessons I started to learn on the training pitches at the Prater stadium as an 18-year-old soldier. Those lessons reached a sort of climax of understanding on a boisterous and very successful trip I made to Budapest with Manchester City four years ago.

We played the faded, once famous Honved in the European Cup-winners Cup and won smoothly, 4-0. Bell was especially good and after the game one Honved official came up to me and said: "That was the best football we have seen from an English club in our country. You showed a lot of skill and a lot of strength and aggression." I was introduced then to the mystique and the background of that extraordinary Hungarian team which burst across Europe in the fifties; it was explained, with great pride, how the left foot power of Puskas developed and how Kocsis became such a deadly header of the ball.

They took me to the little restaurant where I gathered Puskas laid the basis for that famous 'pot', and the house with a red chimney where he lived and which remains, despite his defection during the revolution, a shrine to Hungarian football.

They told me how Puskas made his left foot such a deadly weapon, something so easy and natural that he could control a football as another man holds a fountain pen. And of how Kocsis learned to head the ball with a staggering accuracy. From the age of 16 they used to pool their scraps of money and send Puskas's father, the trainer, down to his

162

favourite wine bar. And while he was away they would practice for hour upon hour. Puskas volleyed the ball endlessly, and Kocsis wuld be there meeting each one with his head. On the rough training pitch beside a railway track Hungarian football was being revolutionised by two kids with great talent and the will to draw upon it.

I was entranced by the stories of the Hungarians. I could see elements in what they were saying which were totally foreign to the English football man. It struck me grimly that English football could not point to one player who had been trained and coached with similar greatness. Of course we have had a profusion of great players, Matthews, Finney, Haynes and Charlton but I believe they reached their stature despite our system not because of it. We have many diamonds in English football, but how many of them are properly polished? At this stage I believe we have only two potentially World-class players in England, Alan Hudson of Stoke City and Trevor Francis of Birmingham.

That is a scanlalously low return from our natural resources. Certainly it suggests to me the need for a total re-think on our coaching techniques, and my plans owe much to that informal academy in an industrial suburb of Budapest. I believe that a club's coaching resources have to be increasingly geared to the needs of the four or five exceptional players at their disposal. Each of these players will have one special talent, maybe a powerful left foot, or an instinct for getting into good positions to head the ball. And these strengths have go be worked on to a much greater extent. The work has to be more intense and there must be a lot of repetition. Out of this you can develop the super player, people whose special skill lifts the team and intimidates the opposition.

In England we have been too sloppy. We do things out of habit and without properly enquiring about their value. There is not the deep conditioning which is an inbuilt thing on the continent and in South America. These are broad outlines of my thinking but I know it is the area where my own hopes of the future will be decided.

Perhaps the track suit days are over for us. It is an important thing in life to realisé when the time comes to move on, and I accept that there is a limit to what you can bring to one field of work. You run the danger of losing impact, of falling back on old methods which you may no longer be able to freshen with enthusiasm.

I recognise that it is time for me to expand my thinking from the tight field of coaching, but I also realise that it will always remain the crucial area of a football club. I see my challenge now as one of direction and emphasis, of adjusting the details of a very specialised coaching drive.

I'm excited, deeply so, about the possibilities. If football is a battle I believe the area of conflict is widening for me. And the spoils of war promise to be that much more satisfying.

# Chapter Sixteen

## The rebel

In December 1970 I was caught in a pincer movement involving the two elements in football upon which I had poured most scorn. The result was a two-month ban from the game. The disaster occurred at Burnley, the fiefdom of that famous pork butcher and self-appointed guardian of football, Bob Lord. At half-time in a match which my Manchester City team were winning comfortably I remarked to referee, Bob Matthewson, a former professional player: "Are you a homer, Bob?" It was a flippant comment stemming from the fact that my team had failed to win one award from Matthewson. It was perhaps a foolish thing to say, but it was said without heat, in a bantering manner. I was scarcely on edge. We were winning 2-0 and only an earthquake could have shaken us out of our rhythm.

But the remark was heard by Burnley officials and it was passed on to Lord. Later in the afternoon Matthewson told me that he would have to report me. I knew I was in deep trouble. I was just a few days away from emerging from a period of suspended sentence. But when the sentence came it was not without value. Though I was taken away from the planning of City's attempt to retain the European

Cup-winners Cup—we lost in a semi-final to Chelsea—it did represent the final, persuasive lesson on the futility of arguing with referees.

I suppose that futility was always apparent to me, right from the early days in Plymouth when I first got into trouble for telling a BBC interviewer that I considered 80 per cent of referees 'homers'. My disciplinary record is appalling. I have been banned from the touch-line for life. I have served one- and two-month suspensions, and the fines I have paid could finance a small private army.

It is a record which says little for my sense of self-preservation. And it says even more for my contempt for men who are given God-like powers. I accept that there has to be a final decision, right or wrong. But what has appalled me, and continues to do so, is the vast and widening gap between the referee and the professionals around him.

It is right that the referee has absolute power. But it is totally wrong that he should be allowed onto a football pitch so obviously ill-equipped for his role. The great majority of referees are fit neither physically nor mentally for the challenge of controlling a high-speed game of professional football. So many of them do not even know how to use their linesmen correctly. And given the fact that so many of them are unfit to keep up with the play the results are often disastrous. They are also the one section of football apparently immune from criticism. It is the ultimate sin to criticise a referee, and the result of this is an unhealthy smugness amongst the majority of match officials.

I do not intend to dwell on this subject. It is a crucial one, I know, but it is also painful. I would not like to calculate the number of times I've left a football ground feeling that my week's work has been wiped away by the blunders of a referee. You might say that such things have a way of levelling off; that to blame a match official is always the easy way out, and that if you are good enough you will surmount all obstacles. In fact it is not as simple as that. Football played well is about fine calculation, about taking the offside law to its refinements, about doing things which depend on a correct interpretation of the rules. Place into such an exercise a man who is either not fit enough to keep pace with the game or not mentally tough enough to grasp the significant points then the whole exercise becomes a frustrating lottery.

Of course there are rare and shining exceptions. I thought Jack Taylor, the butcher from the Midlands, had a superb World Cup Final in Munich in 1974. He was everything a good referee should be, sharp, decisive, and very aware of his linesmen. Yet he came to Crystal Palace and refused a penalty which was embarrassingly obvious. Had the offence been committed anywhere but in a penalty area there would have been no question about the whistle being blown. Such incidents leave you limp with anger. But to protest, to argue, is to invite some elderly gentlemen at the Football Association to cast you out of football. The referee has become a God. To criticise him has become the great heresy.

I suppose some would say that I should have no quarrel with my touch-line ban, that is is something which has probably been imposed for my own good. But I reject this. I do not see why it is wrong for a coach to attempt to influence his team during a game. If he has done his work well in the days before the game his men have a clear and coherent pattern of play, but often an individual can upset that pattern. And on one man a whole club's efforts can collapse. It is as though the authorities are saying: "Well, all right, you can be as professional and as scientific as you like through the week, but once the game starts, forget it." In fact the element of touch-line coaching can add much to the colour and theatre of football. I'm not suggesting for a moment that a match can be won anywhere but out on the field of play, but there is vital information to be transmitted to the pitch. So often you have the ridiculous picture of a manager or coach dangling a piece of bandage as a slim piece of cover for some touch-line coaching.

Why the pretence, the transparent kidology? Is it shameful that a football team responds to the urgent promptings of a man who has spent his whole life in the professional game? Is it right that a schoolmaster or an accountant has the power to dismiss him to the dug-out as though he were correcting an errrant schoolboy?

I should say quickly that at times I did act outrageously on the touch-line. In the atmosphere of success in my first months at Plymouth Argyle I used to play unashamedly to the gallery, leaping out of the dug-out and trampling on my hat or coat if a decision went against us. The crowd used to enjoy themselves; it became part of their afternoon's sport, but from the distance of a few years I'm ready to admit that I was perhaps a bit misguided. The FA must have tired of warning me. I had a series of touch-line arguments with people like John Osborne, Bob Windle, Norman Callender, and incidents with Jim Carr and Peter Rhodes led to a month's ban and the order never to sit again on the touch-line.

The touch-line ban can be a humiliating business. I felt it acutely during the 1969 Cup Final. By swopping tickets I managed to get a seat closer to the pitch, in fact, than the trainers bench. That worked well enough, but in our moment of triumph I felt a cold douse. I leaped over the barrier to join the players, but some stewards grabbed me and hustled me away. It was only when Joe Mercer and some of the players saw what was happening that I was rescued. It was a sharp reminder of the cost of flouting football authority.

I have absorbed the lessons fully now. I can walk away from trouble. Like the successive blows of a hammer, the decisions of the FA disciplinary commissions have taught me that I cannot win. And if I'm honest I have to admit that the manner I went about things meant that I did not deserve to win. I lost control too many times. My urge to win, to

168

announce myself, became a bit of a monster and I was fortunate to have a man of Joe Mercer's weight and influence around at the most monstrous moments.

Having said that, I am not about the join the ranks of the establishment. English football authority is still in a pitiful condition. There is so much reform needed that one hesitates to know where to start. One launching pad might be an attack on the fossilised administration of the Football League and the Football Association. They are supposedly independent bodies but they are interwined in a weird fashion, like Siamese twins not over-fond of each other's company. And always you sense the rule of the amateur. The inflated, Bob Lord-figure, who brings to the game the relative simplicities of selling pies or green-groceries. I have to admit that Lord's club, Burnley, stands out as a fine example of good management in the game. But I also know that it has so much to do with the brilliant pattern laid down by Alan Brown, one of the great post-war English managers.

What English football needs above all is a new breed of men who can grasp fully the potential and the colour of the game. They have to be men of big ideas who can create for themselves the machinery which makes real action possible. The FA made a move in the right direction when they appointed Ted Croker as their secretary. Here is a man who played professional football, who made a great success in business, and who is in touch with the realities of today. But he carries on his back a vast, unwieldy organisation dominated by old men several light years away from the heart of modern football.

The Football League is the organisation which fought Sir Matt Busby's decision to enter European Soccer. The Secretary, Alan Hardaker, was the man at the helm then, and just two years ago his position had scarcely advanced. He offered the opinion that England's exclusion from the World Cup would be forgotten by the public in 'six weeks'. It was an astonishing statement from a man supposedly at the heartbeat of England football.

Such incidents only confirm the need for both bodies to be merged into a new, streamlined directorate, a body which will look at and respond to the needs of the game as a whole.

Only then will it be possible to get the sort of logical decisions which have become commonplace elsewhere. I'm thinking about sharply reduced leagues, so that footballers in England can step off treadmills and into a routine which allows them to refine their skills. I'm thinking about big-budget planning for World Cup attempts, abandonment of league programmes when an international game is imminent. Such things have long been established in places like Brazil and Italy. England manager Don Revie is now attempting to bring in some basics of planning for the national team. And he is appealing, to someone like Hardaker, for co-operation. It is absurd. Revie should not be appealing. He should be demanding.

I have been brought before the FA disciplinary commissions more times than I care to recall. And no doubt in many cases I have been guilty. Sometimes I have even admitted so. My most regular crime? Using abusive, sometimes foul, language to match officials.

What sometimes interests me is when the rulers of English football will themselves be put into the dock. Their crime? We could start with appalling neglect of the interests of English football.

# Chapter Seventeen

## Those I respect

My journey through football has been mostly a solo flight, and deliberately so. Not too many people have made me stand back and say: "You have got something I want to know about." There was Mercer of course. I was glad to stand in the shelter of his influence for five years, and nothing could have been better than that time.

I have also felt respect for men with whom it would have been impossible for me to work. I couldn't get along with a Shankly, for instance. I recognise his tremendous strength, his freakish enthusiasm, but I couldn't see any point at which our thoughts would meet. There is much about Ron Greenwood's work at West Ham which I admire deeply. When he arrived at Upton Park from Arsenal he had a touch of excellence about his work. He knew that his basis would always be deep skill, and that is just about the most vital thing a football man can bring to the game. But there is a vast difference in our styles. The same is true of Dave Sexton, another man whose feelings for the game I respect.

But I have come to regard such men as exceptional. Football may be the greatest of games, but it also offers the weak, the indifferent, and the frankly useless an incredible degree of comfort and cover. There is no logical explanation for the eminence of some football people. Some rise to the top because they are bland, clever politicians; others by a process of good luck and circumstances which defy logic.

And there are others, with infinitely more knowledge, instinct, and perhaps even courage, who are ultimately broken by the game. I'm thinking particularly of the seven men with whom I would have most liked to work had Joe Mercer not taken me on one side in the summer of 1965.

Some of them have shown extraordinary ability in organising and developing teams, some of them have reached out to astonishing moments of success. But all of them have finished looking desperately for answers, their life's work spread by the erratic winds which blow through the game. I'm thinking of Arthur Rowe, Ted Drake, Peter Doherty, George Smith, Bill Nicholson, Alan Brown, and Sir Matt Busby.

I do not think it presumptuous to say I believe I could have prolonged the first rank managerial careers of all these men. I did it with Joe Mercer and I see in this other group of men the same sort of depth and quality which I first encountered in Mercer.

Consider their records, the impact of their work and then their ultimate disillusion.

Rowe, a man of great charm and easy personality, launched the push-and-run Spurs, a team of subtlety and bite who opened the fifties with a flash of brilliance. He did his work with shrewdness and flair. He showed how he could organise and how he could bring to a team that crucial touch of inspiration.

Now, when the game languishes, when the First Division can boast of no more than two or three genuinely inventive teams and when the overall standard lags appallingly, there is no place for Rowe. There is, apparently, no place for one of the great pioneers of modern English football. Yet he remains spry and healthy, and as deeply involved in the theory of the game as he was when he went to Hungary before the war. It is a strange waste.

I see Ted Drake as he goes about his work for Fulham and I think that football has sold another good man short. He built a superb young side at Chelsea, the team Tommy Docherty inherited in its entirety. It was a major performance and it should have placed him nearer the front rank of football management. I feel a certain amount of sympathy for Ted Drake, but I feel more respect. I'm sure he is doing a good job for his club now. But again I cannot escape the feeling that another crucial talent has been discarded.

Peter Doherty, the man I most admired as a player, is quiet, shrewd, and full of ideas. He built a sound Doncaster Rovers team and as Northern Ireland manager he had a dramatic success in the 1958 World Cup finals. But football has put him on a rack. Ultimately he couldn't live with its instability. Yet there should be places for such men.

Men, too, like George Smith who never enjoyed spectacular triumphs as a manager, but did good, solid work at Crystal Palace and Portsmouth. Smith always impressed me as someone who could make a decision, who had a clear idea of his priorities. The current Arsenal coach Bobby Campbell, who did much early work with the present Queen's Park Rangers side, owed much to the guidance and touch of Smith.

I'm sure I would have fought and argued with Alan Brown. My knowledge of him, and all that I have heard about him, suggests to me that he is a very aloof and possibly difficult man. But you can feel a deep strength about him and his record at Burnley was superb. He laid down the foundations of a small club which has ensured their survival in the First Division when all the economic pressures are against them. He too is a man who, for all his deep knowledge—he was one of the first to take European ideas on coaching seriously—has found himself eased away from any influence in English football. It is a catalogue of waste—and last season's ending of the Bill Nicholson reign at White Hart Lane was still another example of the game ultimately rejecting a man who had served it brilliantly.

Nicholson of course had a marvellous reign at White Hart Lane. He won the double, the Cup-winners Cup, with a team that blazed with class. He provided colour and iron, and the balance was perfect. Yet, ultimately, he needed help. The manner of his leaving White Hart Lane, even though his team had been competing in the final of the UEFA Cup just a few months previously, represented a defeat—and it was a defeat all the heavier to bear after what had gone on before.

I think I could have worked with Nicholson in a very productive way. He once said to me that the working life of a football coach at any one club was 18 months. I didn't agree with him but I could see his point. He is the sort of man who has strong thoughts about the game, but he doesn't close his mind to ideas. What happened to him in his last year or so at Tottenham, and possibly to his assistant Eddie Baily, was that a gap appeared between himself and a new generation of players. It is this area of communication which becomes so crucial. But that is not to say that Bill Nicholson's value diminished. His strength did not evaporate.

There was a time, when Sir Matt Busby had twice failed to install a successor, Wilf McGuinness and Frank O'Farrell having lost their jobs, when some people speculated that he might offer me the post of team manager. It was idle speculation, even though Busby had once said to me that if I had coached for him he would have been a manager until he was 70. Busby knew that I had caused much of the pressure that had built around him. But he wouldn't recognise that. He never came to me. He knew that such a move would cause shudders in Manchester. I can only say that the prospect of working with such a big man would have carried immense appeal.

I have been talking about the aristocracy of football men in this country. They are different characters, with different strengths and weaknesses, but to me they have a common bond. Each of them has transmitted to me a good feeling about the game. They have lifted it in my eyes. And if the game has discarded some of them, and deeply frustrated others, that does not reflect on them. They have brought originality and great effort to a game which can obscure talent and elevate the merely bright or opportunistic.

My tribute to them is the simple one that in all the arrogance and self-confidence of my own career I have from time to time recognised that certain people have had about them a special quality and insight. Meeting and talking with such people can be a revealing and sometimes humbling experience, especially when some success may have convinced you that you know all the answers. Joe Mercer once said: "Malcolm has stopped listening and that's bad for any man in the game." He wasn't quite right but I did feel the strength of his remark.

My experiences at Crystal Palace have reinforced that feeling that there is always something fresh to learn about going into a tight situation and making the right decisions. I have also learned the value of delegating duties and working closely with people who have their own ideas and their own particular strength. I am forging, for instance, a partnership with Terry Venables. I believe he is the first of a new generation of key football people. And I have to hope the game will value this generation more keenly than the one that has become lost on the fringes of these critical days.

# Chapter Eighteen

## For God's sake, it's only a silly game

One night last winter I drove numbly up from Selhurst Park to my flat in Kensington. It was a cold, wet, hostile night. When I got into the flat I slumped into a chair. I felt crumpled. My team had lost. The weekend, the flat, my life, was suddenly desolate. Serena, my girlfriend, who is usually very patient, threw a magazine onto the floor and said: "For God's sake, it's only a silly game."

She was both perfectly right and absolutely wrong. The silliness, the futility of football has been evident to me a thousand times. Yet it has been, and I know it always will be, the colour and the rhythm of my life. Without it I know that I'm incomplete. It is difficult, though, to explain to someone who is not so involved how it is to go into a tense battle once, sometimes twice, a week, and how this sensation becomes as important as the air you breathe. You cannot list precisely all those feelings that begin to regulate your life. There is the throbbing that comes in your chest, the prickly sensation at the back of your scalp, and a hundred more.

Certainly as I re-trace the outline of my life the memories and the emotions which lay greatest claim are to do with the silly game. It is like a mistress who tempts you gently, and then down the months becomes so demanding that the mere possession of your body and your time is not enough. That may sound inflated, absurd. But the obsession is real enough. It can be a bit disturbing.

Last year my father died. I loved him not only because he was my father but also because he was a good one, who had given me all he could, including much affection. His death came suddenly, so quickly that one didn't have too much time to think about it. I felt a strange sensation of being empty inside. I noticed people crying at the funeral and I wondered why I didn't feel the same level of emotion. Certainly I felt a great loss. I regretted too that I had not seen as much of him as I would have liked. A lot of things had been left unsaid. I wondered vaguely whether football, though it is in a large sense an artificial thing, does not drain away normal emotions. So that when the time comes to feel something fundamental there is not too much there. I know that I can be a cold, ruthless person, but I also know that I'm capable of much feeling, much love, and the emptiness at my father's funeral made me look at myself in a new way. I'm not sure about any of this. But I have raised certain questions with myself.

The tensions of football bite hardest at the coach or manager. A player can release some of his tension with physical work. He can gather himself and act. A manager or coach—unless he is very strong, has a good sense of perspective or doesn't care enough—sits and suffers. How he carries pressure, whether he channels it creatively or allows it to break his will, depends on his character and his temperament. Sir Matt Busby once told me that he could never, not even when he had Roger Byrne, Duncan Edwards, and Tommy Taylor playing for him, be sure of a victory. He confessed to a tightening of the stomach muscles, a dryness in the mouth. He also told me of the time his team won 6-0 away from home and of how he sought out the home manager after the game, and found him alone in his office with a bottle of scotch. The beaten manager said to Matt, "This game drives you either to drink or an early grave—and I'm too young to die."

I wouldn't put it as strongly as that, but that man's reaction is scarcely rare. The game almost broke the health of a highly intelligent man like Joe Mercer. It cut George Best off at adolesence. It has the power to destroy because it releases unnatural forces. It creates an unreal atmosphere of excitement and it deals in elation and despair and it bestows these emotions at least once a week.

Even for a player who is stable and experienced there can be murderous pressure. One match that I played in, for instance, will live with me always. It was a sixth round FA Cup tie I played for West Ham at Tottenham. For three or four hours before the game I experienced a marvellous sense of anticipation. I longed for the game to start. I felt good and in perfect control. And when I ran out on to the White Hart Lane pitch and looked up at the great stands, crammed with a crowd of 70,000, my feelings were even more heightened. Then, as we kicked about before the start, I felt the strength drain away from me. It took a great effort to put one foot in front of the other. My legs felt rubbery. I wondered if I was going to faint. Only when the referee called me up to the centre circle did I regain control. As I tossed up I felt the strength creeping back into my body. It was the most incredible sense of relief.

There was another wave of tension, though, at half time. I had a fierce row with John Bond, now manager of Norwich City. We were winning 3-2 and I sensed that we were into the semi-finals. I stressed to Bond, an adventurous player who loved to go galloping up on overlaps, that it was absolutely vital that he kept close to Tottenham's left winger, George Robb.

I said to Bond, "Make it simple, keep tight on Robb and just play early balls up to the front players." Bond was close to me and I thought I had got the message through. But without any warning he went careering away down the flank. Robb brought the ball away from him and we were suddenly stretched. I decided to go out to take Robb and was reassured by the fact that Noel Cantwell was behind me. But as I moved towards the winger I was unaware that Cantwell had collided with Bobby Smith and was lying unconscious. I turned in horror as Robb crossed the ball. Len Duquemin was all on his own in front of the goal. He scored and we lost the replay. I still remind John Bond about that. We remain good friends. But he knows I'll never forgive him.

Those moments at White Hart Lane represent the extreme of tension, but it is always there and you have to learn to use it, as you do adrenalin. Sometimes as the team coach swings into a ground and you are due to play an especially important game the throbbing in your chest can become too much. And that is not a nice feeling. But once you are in the dressing room you have your work to do. You have to relax the players in a creative way. You have to stimulate the players and get them into the mood of being a team, conscious of each other and wanting to help and share the effort. You also have to convey the excitement of 'going over the top'. Bill Nicholson's assistant Eddie Baily has been sniped at for such allusions and maybe his attitude became a little fixed in another time, when men responded more easily to such encouragement. But I know the thoughts that must have run through his mind when he tried to drive Spurs out of their decline in recent seasons.

I don't know any feeling to compare with the one you get when you know that the team is going out perfectly prepared. It is a feeling of being re-born. All the mistakes of the past are wiped away. You have built something again and you are going to win. I lost that feeling towards the end of my stay at Manchester City and for a time I struggled to regain it at Crystal Palace. When it didn't come to me naturally I knew that something was wrong. And when you have won you no longer deal in terms of the team. You talk to individuals. You say to each man what is appropriate to his performance. It is a time of special appreciation, not a time for bland comments which go nowhere near the heart of the matter. You measure praise so that it means something. I remember once at West Ham we won a Cup tie against Huddersfield very convincingly. The dressing room was full of directors. I knew I had played well. I sat on the bench with my head between my legs. I was very tired, the pitch had been very heavy. The chairman said: "Well done, Malcolm." I didn't take any notice. Maybe that was ill-mannered, but I couldn't help feeling that gushing praise was out of place. It shouldn't be hinged so strongly to one good performance. Eventually, the chairman said, "I'm talking to you, Malcolm." I said: "Thank you." Certainly the great feeling is when you have got the team on their toes and you are sure about them, to say: "Okay, let's go, babies"—and then later, when you have won, there is the separate feeling of satisfaction.

And then there is Sunday morning. The ground of a winning club is never deserted on a Sunday morning. Invariably, a few players will turn up for a bit of treatment. They are prepared, happy, to show themselves. When the team has lost the place is deserted. I remember in the early days at Manchester City how the players used to come into the ground with their heads down—and how they couldn't get away from the place quickly enough. It is all, I suppose, basic human nature and perhaps the extraordinary and compulsive thing about football is that it heightens all your emotions. There are not many ways of life which require a weekly examination in public, a test of courage and skill and even simple adequacy.

The pressure of defeat can force you into behaviour you can regret deeply. In the spring of 1972 Manchester City lost a night match at Ipswich and with it the title. The team were travelling back to London after the game but I did not join them in the team coach. My old racing friend Arthur Shaw drove me away from the ground. I didn't want to get involved in any recriminations with the players. But I should have gone with them. They had not let me down. I learned something about taking defeat that night. It hurt me very deeply and I didn't react as well as I would have liked.

But I tell myself that the important thing is to do my work as well as I can and always try to turn every situation into an advantage. I believe you can become very strong at the places where you have appeared to be most weak. And if I have conveyed at times an excess of confidence, much of it has been a necessary act.

I remember a man taking me down for a trial at Charlton Athletic. I was fifteen and terribly unsure of myself. I didn't feel big enough or good enough, but I played centre forward, scored three goals, and was signed by Charlton. I recall a war-time game at the Valley when I was called to the ground and told to stand by. Charlton were playing Arsenal, who had Boy Bastin in their team. One of our players, George Green, was late and I was told that if he had not turned up within five minutes I was going out there. I felt a terrible fear right up to the moment Green arrived—and I have tried never to lose the memory of that fear. I have also tried never to lose the memory of how difficult it could be to play well, nor the crushing effect on a player when a manager comes into the dressing room and criticises him for failing to control a certain ball. Of course one fails. But it is important at least to fight yourself at moments of extreme disappointment, to remember how trickily a ball can pitch in front of your feet, or how one fractional mis-timing can cause havoc.

There are times, too, when you have to work hard at building your own confidence. After my illness I was aware that a lot of aggression and buoyancy had gone out of me. I had to work at being a character, which is not the best thing. At Bath I bought myself a Russian hat. At Plymouth I once waved to the directors to salute me after we had scored a two-touch penalty. Absurd touches, I suppose, but they seemed to be necessary to me then. I was trying to fill a vacuum in myself.

Gradually the game and my success in it stripped away some of that artificial side. I have been able to get back some of that simple excitement which came to me when I saw my first floodlit game as a boy. It was at Highbury. I had never seen grass so green. The shirts of the players were so vivid.

And the game can bring unexpected rewards. One of my greatest thrills came when Francis Lee swept Manchester City into the League Cup Final with a flash of the unorthodox which left Manchester United floundering. We were awarded an indirect free kick, for which I had laid down elaborate plans in training. But Lee hammered the ball at goal, I said 'idiot', and then watched Alex Stepney, the United keeper, palm the ball down into the path of one of our forwards. Success in football is lined with such freakish feats.

And with the rewards, the constant inter-play of triumph and disappointment, and the great, churning excitement, there is the price you have to pay. I have never been able to calculate this. The game demands total involvement and the first, most obvious cost is in human relationships. It has kept me away from people I have loved. It has led me to take advantage of people, good, sincere people, and it has never given me the time that a man properly needs to examine himself. I am learning about this now.

Football has only once, and very briefly, offered me security. That was when some Manchester City directors talked about giving me a 20-year contract. It never materialised of course, and in a way I'm grateful for that. I think if I had security, or if I began to think in terms of it, my attitude would change and I would become, at least to myself, less of a man. Once when I was young, a colleague, a goalkeeper called Peter Chiswick, suggested I join the freemasons. He told me it would be a good idea and that it would help my future. He was to propose me at a forthcoming Lodge meeting. But he died suddenly. I never got to join the freemasons and again I do not mourn that

182

fact. I believe in individuals. I value the team effort, as any football man must, but I think it has limits. And if I get on I want to feel that it is because of my own efforts and not because I moved with the right people and got help at the right times.

I have to accept that at the age of 47 my career is poised quite delicately now. I am working for the big achievement, which if accomplished could determine the shape of the rest of my life. I want to build something important at Crystal Palace. And some days I get a terrible impatience for the old glory days. I don't like to see my team's match reports low down in the national newspapers. I get a terrible hunger for the big match, the big throb in the chest.

I'm also conscious that the defeats and the set-backs at Crystal Palace can ultimately be turned to my advantage. But if they are not, if a gap appears between my ambitions and their fulfilment, and should I, say, get the sack, I'm not likely to run for cover. I know, whatever happens, that I have got something inside me. That may sound like arrogance, and if so that is just too bad. I've learned that it is possible to live off centre stage if you have made it once, however you have achieved that—and however fleeting the time you spent there.

Many people have said things to me, and about me, since I slipped into the Third Division. But they have been involved in a pseudo-fight, against an opponent contemptuous of the conflict.

I have proved certain things to myself and that is what a man needs most of all.

If I need anything from the game at large and the people I have known it is perhaps only the acknowledgement that there have been times when I have gone in and fought for things I considered important.

Maybe I have left some things unsaid, and no doubt some of the achievements I seek will never be fulfilled. But if I go tomorrow, I hope it can be said that I did a few things, and I loved a few people.

# Index

185

189